MW01223600

To Kin...
Here's to ...
peace admist
life's surprises

your friends, and

Diane

"X!"

19.Sept.23

WARNING!

CONTENTS UNDER

PRESSURE

Overcoming the Overload

Rusty Moore

Copyright © 2017 by Rusty Moore

ISBN 978-1-4958-1404-4
ISBN 978-1-4958-1405-1 eBook
Library of Congress Control Number: 2017904665

All Scripture quotations are from the Authorized King James Version of the Bible which is in the public domain.

"Warning Contents Under Pressure" graphic image created by Russell Stutler and used by permission.

Published June 2017

INFINITY PUBLISHING
1094 New DeHaven Street, Suite 100
West Conshohocken, PA 19428-2713
Toll-free (877) BUY BOOK
Local Phone (610) 941-9999
Fax (610) 941-9959
Info@buybooksontheweb.com
www.buybooksontheweb.com

DEDICATION

First and foremost I dedicate this book to the Lord of Hosts Who is and shall always be my personal Lord and Savior. It is by Jesus Christ and Him alone that I have been given knowledge, understanding, and wisdom concerning the revelation of truth in His infallible Word. Without the shadow of a doubt I know that it is the good, acceptable, and perfect will of God that we have quality of life and increase in it continually. Outside of Jesus there is truly no abundant life. Without Him there is no defining purpose to our lives.

When faced with so many troubles, pressures, concerns, and obstacles in life there is only One Who is with me the whole way, One alone that is my best friend. He is Jesus. I pray this book will encourage, uplift, direct, correct, and protect you and those you hold dear. I pray that the Word of the Living God will remain and grow in your heart, never to depart.

I encourage you to meditate upon His Word which has been revealed, never concealed. Let His Word be your desire. Know that when you receive of His truth it will take you higher. Always remember that Jesus is greater, Jesus is stronger, and Jesus is healer.

Warning:

This book contains
Truth, prophecy, and revelation.
Listening to these words
Can and will
Bring salvation!

TABLE OF CONTENTS

BY HIS FRUITS
(A Word of Introduction)

I was reading about Smith Wigglesworth, a remarkable man of God who inspired millions and displayed the faith that causes God to move. Something he said struck me, "A man cannot preach above his own wisdom." He went on to explain that if one has not experienced what he is ministering about, then he cannot effectively impact the hearers.
With that being said, I am much experienced in what I am sharing with you here! In my own life I have faced many trials and tribulations. I know firsthand about battles with fear, sickness, depression, and oppression. I am no stranger to betrayal, resentment, ridicule, persecution, and false accusation. Pressures of all kinds, afflictions, loneliness, tiredness, weakness, and abandonment have all shown up in my life at some point.

Though having experienced these temporary circumstances, there is something that has remained unchanged in my life—the grace and mercy of Jesus Christ. His everlasting strength carries me through, making all things in my life work together for good to me because I love Him and I am the called according to His purpose (Romans 8:28).

I would not have been able to write this book without having had the experience of going through those challenges. From my perspective of having walked out these areas with the Lord, I am telling you that there is love, joy, peace, and hope to help you overcome as well! My suggestion is for you to take heed and not give place to the lies of hell. God's Truth reigns, and it is up to us to allow Him to reign in our hearts, minds, souls, and spirits.

The Warning Label

One thing is quite evident today—people are attracted to what they relate to or feel. So the fact that you even picked up this book is interesting. What's going on inside you that drew you to this title? Feeling stressed? Life in a mess? Or are you just curious? Are you yourself a walking *warning label*? One thing is for sure: it's not too late to change what you might think is the inevitable. As you begin this journey we will take a step-by-step honest look at some crucial factors that will bring you valuable insight and diffuse your current stresses and pressures.

We must begin by realizing that what we feel is often masked by a subtle gesture of socially-acceptable exchanges such as the common smile or the simple question, "How are you?" In the nearly automatic response to that question—"I'm good; how are you?"—we consciously and/or subconsciously express a fear. To answer the question with a real answer might bring a problem to the surface that would then make others uncomfortable and interfere with engaging in further conversation. So we suppress it and give the standard acceptable response.

Hiding in seclusion within the depths of our souls, our minds tend to navigate toward a quieter, less vulnerable resolution. We all have, unfortunately, beheld the circumstances that arise from the secret and hidden pressures that we have faced. The most detrimental attribute to these situations is that more than one person is critically injured, so often bringing destruction to innocent bystanders—our family and friends.

Isn't it ironic that so many times we have seen the warning labels very distinctly marked on pressurized containers, and yet we fail to realize the same warning signs on ourselves? Are we oblivious to the obvious? It could be that we just don't pay attention at this level. Whether we see it as yet or not, there is clearly a relationship between what we hold in

Are we oblivious to the obvious? It could be that we just don't pay attention at this level.

our hand (a container that has been forcefully injected with a mixture of some sort to maximum capacity) and our current mental state. People are containers, are we not? We can hold in what we take in; we can let out what we feel. And just like that we become a container—a dispersing instrument.

So what about those of us whose minds have been forcefully injected and filled from the onslaught of one problem after another, one problem on top of another? Ah! So the pressure of circumstances continues to expand within us, leading us to exhibit a silent label that reads, "Warning! Contents Under Pressure!"

The dangers of reflecting this warning label are quickly seen when we look at it in this way. In reality we are not the only ones wearing this warning label. People all around us—some we know, some we don't know—are dealing with their own pressures, too. They all have their own labels just like ours.

We can see how volatile the situation can become as we mix all these "dangerous containers" together. Not only is there a risk of bringing harm to one's own self, but it is possible, and perhaps even likely, that harm can be irresponsibly brought to those innocent ones around us. When we come to the point of feeling and becoming so overwhelmed, so overtaken and overworked, it will be the innocent that will be overlooked. We have to realize that preventive measures must be set up in order to preserve not only our own lives, but the lives of those we love.

Following the path of being a youth pastor and a substitute teacher has led me into circumstances where I have seen firsthand the affliction of kids living in a consistent, chaotic disruption of despair, oppression, and depression. This young generation of brilliant, passionate, and determined youth is being choked by external and internal pressures that are clouding their minds with constant discouragement and frustration. They become so overwhelmed with pressures from home, school, and life in general that some of them choose to take the path of self-destruction. Drinking, drugs, and sexual behavior become to them a simple way to escape. Sadly, after the constant mental and emotional decline, the storms that rage within their minds lead them to the conclusion that suicide is the only way out. Did you know that nearly one in six high school students seriously consider suicide and one in twelve have actually attempted it?

We are so often driven to escape the pressures of our own perceived thoughts that we forget that this montage only hurls us in a downward spiral ending in tragedy. The word montage means *any combination of different elements that forms or is felt to form a unified whole, single image, etc.* Our own mental picture of what we interpret as a real truth is nothing more than a real lie. So in turn, we tend to lose ourselves in the struggle between escaping and remaining.

The increasing questions of confusion, doubt, frustration, and anger expand within us. This leaves us vulnerable to the lies that seem so overwhelming and so true. The lies cause us to enter into a shallow grave of despair. And thus the declaration is made that *life is unfair, all hope is gone, all is lost*, not realizing that truly, all is yet to be found.

> *So in turn, we tend to lose ourselves in the struggle between escaping and remaining.*

We as individuals are so different, yet we are the same. We are all born with the innate desire to feel and be wanted, to feel and be loved, to feel and be appreciated, to know our destiny and walk in it. Still there remains for millions of people an emptiness that has yet to be filled. In the constant experiencing of trials, tribulations, and tragedy along life's highway, they discover a road that only winds itself in a giant circle. This pathway leaves them with the impression that it is impossible for their lives to change. This thought—this lie—leads to a desperate attempt to seek an exit ramp.

Frustration, anger, and despair overcome the true purpose of millions of people in this present hour. With so much pressure building up inside, hiding from those who are oblivious to our condition (which we think should be so obvious to all), we struggle on in quiet desperation. In this condition how can we possibly find one who will see our hidden tears? Who will hear our silent screams? Or comfort our unexpressed depression? Why is the expressed and very often prideful persona allowed to choke out the very cry for help we so desperately need? Why do we choose to bathe in a sea of despair and darkness when we can bathe in a Heaven filled with joy and light?

Some of the problem lies with the people who think they know us, but don't really know us at all. Problems buried within the realm of our minds tend to hide themselves even in the very best of us, and are frequently masked by common, socially-acceptable gestures such as those mentioned earlier.

But much of the problem falls at our own door. Too often we find ourselves driven by a desire to refrain from allowing others to penetrate the core of our own problems. We don't want them to see our weaknesses, therefore, we put on a display of what we think is strength. We attempt to come off as overcomers, but the sad reality is, because our day-to-day internal struggles are left unattended, we are overcome instead.

I know what it is like to be engulfed
With a raging sea of turmoil on the inside,
Trying to hide it from the outside world.
With sails torn, the hull battered,
My thoughts—a million scattered—
I have come to the place
Where maybe the watery grave
Would actually bring that longed-for peace
From the endless storms that raged within.
I have found myself many times on a distant sea
Sailing in a world of confusion
With a course set,
Trying to find my destiny.
I knew it was out there somewhere,
But *when* I would get there
Continued to be the haunting question.
What is it like to know
There is more to life than what you see?

Every day seems more repetitive
Than the day before—all vanity,
Following the same patterns day after day,
Recognizing the pitfalls of the endless cycle
We have labeled insanity.

The answer is to remain hooked to the Anchor—Jesus—
For when our desire outweighs the norm,
There is the testimony given after the storm.
I have often asked God the question as David did,
"Who am I?"
But I add to his question,
"That You would cause me to live, not die?"
For out of the darkness many times my soul would cry,
Knowing there is only One who could reach down
Farther than I could reach up.
As I was broken inside, hollow, and crumbling into nothing
Jesus would always declare Himself El Shaddai
And overflow my cup.
I have often come to the place of pressure
At the end of my rope,
But somehow, some way,
There would always shine from Him a ray of hope.
I can honestly say that many times in my life,
My faith was tempted to fail,
But one thing was sure—
His Word would always prevail.

~~~~~

[12]Beloved, think it not strange concerning the fiery trial which is to try you, as though some strange thing happened unto you; 1 Peter 4:12

[7]That the trial of your faith, being much more precious than of gold that perisheth, though it be tried with fire, might be found unto praise and honour and glory at the appearing of Jesus Christ: 1 Peter 1:7

With our own perceived notion of failure come the feelings that seem to haunt us with the fear of failing yet again. Frustration comes with disappointment. Anger follows close behind until doubt finally brings us into a pit of despair and helplessness. All this takes place shadowed from the possibility of another person knowing the struggle that we carry.

Millions of people, Christians included, currently exist in a state of burnout due to the absence of yet-to-be-discovered purpose in their lives. It leaves them overwhelmed with no satisfaction as they live the same repetitious cycle day in, day out, year in, year out. They are wanting and grasping for change, but coming to the conclusion that it will always be just beyond reach where they'll never have contact with it.

The dangerous part of harboring despair is that we come too quickly to the false conclusion that *life is not fair*. Subconsciously we are saying, "God, You are not fair." This is the thought of so many today—in churches, in your house, at the grocery store, in the checkout lines, in the parking lots, the theme parks. No matter where you go, there they are. Or dare I say, "There you are!"

Sometimes we deal with failure by letting it set us up for more failures. Sometimes we allow failures to move us toward our own definition of success. Our attitude toward those failures will determine how we come to know who we really are and the potential that lies ahead. We so often tend to be creatures of habit (the familiar), traveling down the worn paths of "accepted success" instead of striking out on new paths to discover the true purpose and potential God has destined for us. This is why it is imperative that His will be your will, too.

> *The dangerous part of harboring despair is that we come too quickly to a false conclusion that life is not fair.*

What I am about to share with you is an excerpt from a message that I preached entitled *Failure to Launch*. Let's begin with a passage found in Luke 5:1-6.

¹And it came to pass, that, as the people pressed upon him to hear the word of God, he stood by the lake of Gennesaret,

²And saw two ships standing by the lake: but the fishermen were gone out of them, and were washing *their* nets.

³And he entered into one of the ships, which was Simon's, and prayed him that he would thrust out a little from the land. And he sat down, and taught the people out of the ship.

⁴Now when he had left speaking, he said unto Simon, Launch out into the deep, and let down your nets for a draught.

⁵And Simon answering said unto him, Master, we have toiled all the night, and have taken nothing: nevertheless at thy word I will let down the net.

⁶And when they had this done, they in closed a great multitude of fishes: and their nets brake.

Jesus gave Peter a command to do something, but Peter's response was the same as that of millions today—*Jesus, I'm tired of doing what I have been doing. I'm tired of tithing. I'm tired of going to church. I'm tired of helping others because when I do it, all I ever seem to get in return is nothing* (which in itself is a wrong motive). *My life is consumed by vanity and insanity, and seemingly the more I press on, the more I feel I'm running on empty.*

I really want you to understand this revelation that the Lord brought to my attention. It is crucial to not only my life, but to yours as well. And that revelation is this: **The opportunity of Simon's lifetime came at a time when he was getting ready to hang it up.** Simon was disgusted, busted, tired, worn out, possibly burned out, frustrated, and discouraged.

Ask yourself this question: Why do you think the enemy wants to get me into this mentality? God gives us a command that relates to this issue. It is a command and not a suggestion.

> ⁹And let us not be weary in well doing: for in due season we shall reap, if we faint not. Galatians 6:9

I was reading in Joel Osteen's book *It's Your Time* about a young man who was hiking up a mountainside. We know the Christian walk can be a hike as well. We all press toward the goal of reaching the top. After a great while of trekking, this young man came to a point where he wanted to quit, wanted to give up and go back down the mountain. But as he began to do just that, he saw another man come from up ahead. As the gentleman passed him he made the comment, "You are closer than you think."

In another prime example, I heard about a man who started looking for gold in a certain area. He just knew the gold was there. He bought all the right equipment and did everything he knew to do for gold prospecting. After pursuing his dream that seemed to become a nightmare, he decided to give up on finding the gold and sold all his equipment. The company that bought him out continued on where he left off. It wasn't very long until they discovered one of the richest gold findings of history.

Listen, there is an appointed time and a season of labor that sometimes lasts longer than what we think it should. In the same way, there is also an appointed time of reaping. This is a Kingdom of God principle. Seed time and harvest go hand in hand. But so often we are discouraged by the pressures of life that we fail to realize the latter part of the promise. So do not give up! Lord knows I have wanted to sometimes, but His grace carried me on because I knew it was nothing of me. It was all Him!

But here is revelation: when you finally come to your end, that's when God can begin, but not until then.

Simon had just experienced great failure. He was doing everything right—after all, he was a professional fisherman. He did everything he knew to do. He knew when to do it, how to do it, and yet, he still experienced failure. His nets were empty. How many times have you been in the same situation as Simon and you say, "God, what am I doing wrong?" But here is revelation: when you finally come to your end, that's when God can begin, but not until then.

When I was,involved in sales at one time, it became customary to offer a positive quote or a motivational thought that would inspire us all in obtaining our personal goals. One morning during the meeting when asked if I had anything to share, I made this statement: *The opportunity of a lifetime must be seized in the lifetime of the opportunity.* It has stuck with me to this day.

Isn't it so true that the flesh is weak, but the spirit is, indeed, willing? Even though Simon felt this way, something was burning on the inside of his heart that caused him to yield. There is no doubt that it was something Jesus had said while teaching. So Simon caught hold of himself and basically said, "No matter what has happened or how I feel, nevertheless, at Thy word I will let down my net."

You have to come to that same point. When all seems to go wrong in your life, when the pressures of the worries are weighing you down, when people are pressuring you to do the opposite of what God says, you must grab hold of yourself and shake yourself to the point of saying, "Nevertheless, God, I will praise You. No matter how I feel or what I'm going through, I am going to worship You. I am going to obey You."

The Greater One on the inside of you will prompt you to do this. Once you do it, all will be well. That is why the enemy presses you so hard until you become oblivious to the obvious solution. The answer is so simple. Satan knows that if you start praising God that God's glory will come down like a mighty flood and cause him to flee, giving you the ultimate victory.

We say, *but I feel so much pain, so much hurt, so much grief...* to the point that we become convinced that lies are truth, and truth is nowhere to be found. Oh, I know that the pain is real and the grief is real. However, Jesus can reveal His everlasting mercy that will encompass you and take you to your breakthrough.

The Arrival

We have all, at some point in our lives, enjoyed the arrival of someone or something new. It might have been a new baby, a new car, a new job or house. With the new experience the presence of joy is birthed forth into our lives. It brings with it an excitement that fills not only the atmosphere, but our relationships, our homes and places of business.

It is evident that we not only experience this rewarding in our lives, but we are also presented with the arrival of circumstances that may propel us into a mode of self-survival. These affect us mentally, physically, emotionally, and even spiritually, whether we realize it or not.

Let's proceed with the following association. If I say the word *pressure* then you say _____. Did you automatically think something like *headache, migraine, weight, burden, stress*? Or was your thought more toward *explode*!

Isn't it obvious that we are living in an ever-changing technological society? The faster the world seems to go, the more we find ourselves feeling obligated to trying to keep up with everything. This is a constant source of mental, physical, emotional, and spiritual breakdowns, and dare I say, break-ups.

Pressure. What is it? Where is it found? How is it used? What causes pressure? What are the results of pressure? Before we answer these questions let's contemplate a certain culprit that brings the *convenience* of so many choices and options into our lives.

Ask yourself this question: Is the availability of so many choices and options a blessing or a curse in my life? Which is simpler, a menu that presents just a specialty course or one that presents a wide array of different foods and preparation styles?

Would you agree that a great many pressures that you have felt have come from the arrival of choices? How often have you voiced these questions?

- What am I going to do?
- How am I going to handle this?
- What are they going to think?
- Who can I get to help me?

The thought that usually accompanies questions of this nature sounds something like *because if I do this then this will happen, but if I don't do that then this could happen, but I could...* On and on it goes. In that way the pressure builds itself upon a foundation of possibilities and unanswered questions.

We are currently dwelling in a time of technological increase that is conforming our minds to a world of instant gratification and satisfaction. The press of a button or a mere voice command can now give us what we want. And if it is not delivered in timely fashion, we find ourselves frustrated. Most of the time it's an insignificant thing, yet it causes pressurized thoughts to build within our minds.

Technology has advanced under the banner of achieving maximum production and maximum efficiency. Yet the pressures that it brings with it have caused us to unwittingly experience a deficiency that has left our precious souls deprived. Instead of more and better, we find ourselves inadequately equipped with what we truly need to be productive. The continual build-up of pressure from the world's influence of "got to have it" has, unfortunately, become our master.

Our thinking that solutions and opportunities should just come at the press of a button or a voice command is programming us to some untruth. Though this easy instant access seems to be in our best interest, I say that it wears a disguise to lead us away from the true characteristics of Who God is and what He expects from those who have been called His own. We are losing such precious revelation. And we question the

The continual build-up of pressure from the world's influence of "got to have it" has, unfortunately, become our master.

one we call God in our times of trouble, wondering how and if He will ever show up. It is sad that the more we think we have in this high-tech world to see and to hear, the more blind and deaf we become.

I dare not speak this as a matter of opinion, but I speak it in truth having observed it in widespread reality. With the epidemic of social disconnection among families, friends, and loved ones it is no wonder that when pressures come people are not prepared to deal with them. The deeper tragedy is not necessarily the results of the pressures that come, but that the pressures themselves could have been diffused by a simple, nearly-forgotten act known as *one-on-one conversation.*

It seems that with technology becoming *smarter* we are becoming *dumber* in some ways—less present. People have become dependent on technology to help them through their everyday routines. There are millions of people who actually say, "I can't live without my phone, laptop, tablet, etc." We are living in very dangerous times where pressures resulting from conflicts around the world are influencing our very thoughts toward a more desperate need of relief. The question that we must ask ourselves is, "What am I going to do if the power goes out?

Here Comes the Pressure

So how is pressure defined? I believe our encounters have directly defined it well enough, but we can still clarify the answer. Pressure is defined as *the weight or force that is produced when something presses or pushes against something else; the burden of physical or mental distress; the constraint of circumstance; the weight of social or economic imposition; the application of force to something by something else in direct contact with it; the stress of urgency of matters demanding attention.*

It is true that none of us, especially Christians, is immune to the susceptibility of pressures. They present themselves in many forms with each sharing a simple common goal: *for one to be rendered useless, to break one down in thought, to crush hope, to destroy dreams, and to mar the senses where the thought of freedom is extinguished.* Remember, what *appears* to be truth in our own mind during a moment of trial and pressure (perceived to be inescapable) is only the illusion from a lie. Through the power of God's word we can cause that lie to forever die!

Pressure has presented itself in our lives through a wide variety of forms, fashions, and fits. I want to peer into a portion of Biblical history and look at one form of pressure that we are all familiar with—the pressure to fear.

> [8]And the Lord hardened the heart of Pharaoh king of Egypt, and he pursued after the children of Israel: and the children of Israel went out with an high hand.
> [9]But the Egyptians pursued after them, all the horses *and* chariots of Pharaoh, and his horsemen, and his army, and overtook them encamping by the sea, beside Pihahiroth, before Baal-zephon.

> ¹⁰And when Pharaoh drew nigh, the children of Israel lifted up their eyes, and, behold, the Egyptians marched after them; and they were sore afraid: and the children of Israel cried out unto the Lord. Exodus 14:8-10

We can literally see that pressure can come, and when it does, sometimes there's a lot of it. This was life or death to them. Notice that in verse 9 the word *overtook* is used. Have you noticed that is a common confession among many people today, including Christians? How many times have you heard Christians talking about how much they are overwhelmed and seemingly overtaken? Jacob makes the statement in Genesis 42:36: *all these things are against me.*

> And Jacob their father said unto them, Me have ye bereaved *of my children:* Joseph *is* not, and Simeon *is* not, and ye will take Benjamin *away:* all these things are against me.

Remember this, when you feel overcome, overwhelmed, and overworked, know that the Word of God is being overlooked. Many of us will desperately search for escape from circumstances of stress and pressure because we are convinced that we cannot handle them. People leave jobs, churches, relationships, and their hometowns hoping to evade future events that will surely bring distress and discomfort.

The Israelites saw the Egyptians coming, and it caused them to feel the pressure of overwhelming anxiety. This caused them to yield to doubt which caused them to speak unbelief toward God. Being full of fear will always cause us to be faith-*less.* And being faith-*full* will cause us to be fear-*less.*

> **When you feel overcome, overwhelmed, and overworked, know that the Word of God is being overlooked.**

Think of a time, maybe in the workplace, where your boss told you to get something done. You know, it's not that you didn't have enough to do already, and here came more. So you began to feel the pressure build because your mind focused on all that had to be done. You kept thinking about it because it was so much to handle. You constantly wondered how in the world you were going to get it all done on time. Then as these thoughts started flooding your mind you began to start thinking about hating the job, hating the people you work with, hating your boss. Then you began complaining about how you never have anyone to help. Before you knew it, you were absolutely ready to explode.

Complaining will always take us far away from the ever-present help of God. It will regretfully drive us into fear, dismay, and foolish actions. Even though God by His mighty hand delivered His people with His great power, something interesting took place within them. They had the privilege of seeing the very Glory of God manifest on their behalf. Still, they soon forgot the precious acts of deliverance, and then faced with the pressure of fear, they began to complain.

I am reminded of a time when I went into a local restaurant. On the counter was an interesting display. It was an unusual way to declare the establishment's rules and guidelines regarding complaints. In bold print on a free-standing sign were the words: *Complaint Department. Take a Number.* What's so unique about that? It was that the next number up for the taking just happened to be connected to the pin on a grenade! It was a dummy grenade, of course, but it made its point well.

I can picture humorously in my mind those times when all the people would go to Moses with their problems. He probably would have loved to have had something similar for those people! The fact is, no one enjoys hearing another complain about circumstances. It is nothing more than a breeding ground for negativity which draws in evil spirits. Those spirits continue to further that realm in order to manifest more of themselves. The influence of those evil spirits takes people away from the promises of God. The spirits know and recognize that He is mightier than they, but they will do their best to deafen the hearer to keep him or her from listening to what God is saying.

We may think sometimes that our jobs are really bad, but just think how bad it would have been in Moses' shoes. In Exodus 18:13, 17-18 we read the following:

> [13]And it came to pass on the morrow, that Moses sat to judge the people: and the people stood by Moses from the morning unto the evening.
> [17]And Moses' father in law said unto him, The thing that thou doest *is* not good.
> [18]Thou wilt surely wear away, both thou, and this people that *is* with thee: for this thing *is* too heavy for thee; thou art not able to perform it thyself alone.

Why is it that we seem to have this notion that we alone are to somehow fix our problems, other people's problems, and create forms of resolution in worlds of conflict? People will always tend to gravitate toward other people for advice, for comfort, for love, for peace, for whatever, desiring a quick resolution. I am not saying that is bad, but when it is done constantly over and over, then I believe for the most part we are missing God.

We must recognize the amount of pressure that Moses faced when leading this great multitude. The constant complaining, rebelling, betraying, and bickering that he dealt with daily was enough to drive the normal man into a realm of insanity. It is apparent that it was so bad with the Israelites that God came to the point where He didn't even call them His people anymore. He called them Moses' people! God and Moses actually went back and forth over this!

> [7]And the Lord said unto Moses, Go, get thee down; for **thy** people, which **thou** broughtest out of the land of Egypt, have corrupted *themselves:*
> [11]And Moses besought the Lord his God, and said, Lord, why doth thy wrath wax hot against **thy** people, which **thou** hast brought forth out of the land of Egypt with great power, and with a mighty hand?
> Exodus 32: 7, 11

What I see here is a discussion, a debate. Moses, knowing the situations that erupted within this group of people, rebuts the statement of God with the following modern-day response, *Oh no God! Them ain't my peoples! Them be your peoples! You ain't putting them on me!*

But the problem was that Moses was trying to do it alone. God had not designed him to do that. God has not designed any of us to carry such burden. That is God's job! There's something huge to learn from this in our own day and time.

Pastors of all sorts are making this very mistake today. If you are a pastor, a father, a mother, or a leader of any kind within the body of Christ, listen to what Jethro, Moses' father-in-law, had to say. Do not think that you alone are able to carry the burdens of your congregation or your family. Do not feel pressured into thinking it is your obligation to listen to everyone's problems, complaints, or concerns in order to make everything alright.

God gave Jethro the wisdom to apply to Moses' situation, and there is wisdom for your situation, too. Failing to yield to Jethro's advice would have caused a wicked device to prosper, and Moses would have ended up emotionally, physically, and spiritually dead.

The Master has given us His own word for every season in our lives. When we fail to listen to such simple truth we find ourselves in the constant turmoil of oncoming stress. This ultimately causes pressure to build up inside that damages our bodies and our precious minds. Thoughts whose origins are not in God flood our minds, heaving upon us a great weight of discouragement, despair, and dread that only seems to worsen with time. And as that process takes place, we are still attempting to eradicate on our own the situation that only He can resolve.

Jesus declared unto us the following commandment in Matthew 11:28-30:

> 28Come unto me, all *ye* that labour and are heavy laden, and I will give you rest.
> 29Take my yoke upon you, and learn of me; for I am meek and lowly in heart: and ye shall find rest unto your souls.
> 30For my yoke *is* easy, and my burden is light.

Are you a boater or do you have a friend who enjoys a boat? There can be so much excitement and anticipation of the fun activities to come! But there is one key element to preventing a disaster and state of panic, and that is remembering to put the drain plug back in before you launch! Soon and very soon the realization comes that it's either bail or sink!

I'm sure you would agree with me that the most dreaded time to be out on the water is when a storm arises. The strong winds can hurl massive waves against the boat. It can reach the point where the vessel can be overtaken with water. It's a dangerous situation and very stressful.

It is in the gospel of Mark that we read about one of these incidents arising in the lives of Jesus and His disciples. Let's take a look into their boat.

> [35]And the same day, when the even was come, he saith unto them, Let us pass over unto the other side.
> [36]And when they had sent away the multitude, they took him even as he was in the ship. And there were also with him other little ships.
> [37]And there arose a great storm of wind, and the waves beat into the ship, so that it was now full.
> [38]And he was in the hinder part of the ship, asleep on a pillow: and they awake him, and say unto him, Master, carest thou not that we perish? Mark 4:35-38

In Luke's account of this same storm, he said it this way:

> [23]But as they sailed he fell asleep: and there came down a storm of wind on the lake; and they were filled with water, and were in jeopardy. Luke 8:23

What is taking place in this scenario is actually called the law of displacement. The once nearly empty air space is displaced with an unstoppable flow of water that eventually causes enough weight and pressure that the vessel can no longer hold itself above the water. This displacement thus begins the descent of the vessel, causing those on board to panic in an overwhelming fear. A chaotic demise is possibly imminent.

With this analogy of the wooden vessel taking on water in the natural, we as earthen vessels of spirit, soul, and body are susceptible to the same outcome. We too often listen to the voice of false presumption that there is just so much coming into and going on in our lives that there is no possible way of escape. This presumptive thinking creates an invitation of defeat which can include depression, nervous breakdowns, drinking binges, drug addiction, massive amounts of prescription medications, and even suicide.

Even the disciples in the boat with Jesus during that storm came to the point of drawing a false conclusion.

A man who owned a tobacco shop was asked how his business was doing. The owner replied, "Really good! Everyone is so stressed out by the economy that people are smoking a lot more now."

Even the disciples in the boat with Jesus during that storm came to the point of drawing a false conclusion. They looked at the "overwhelming" evidence around them that told them they were doomed, that this was the end. I have to say it again here, *when you feel overwhelmed, overtaken, and overworked, then the Word of God is being overlooked.*

With so many thoughts about the endless possibilities that can occur at any given moment in time, we can easily find ourselves engulfed in a whirlwind of agonizing mental torment. There is a prevalent worldly mentality plaguing our way of life. It says that we must keep up with the ever-changing technological advances that are introduced to us on practically a daily basis. In this mentality, multi-tasking is a necessity, a skill to be exercised with great precision and speed. The constant goal? To further productivity and meet the margins that must be met. Is this really working?

What can actually be the most productive is something quite different. It is rather the ability to become still, not just bodily, but especially mentally. In my own experience of facing this realm of mental torment, I hear the Word of God arise within my spirit saying, "Be still and know that I am God" (Psalm 46:10).

> [3]Thou wilt keep *him* in perfect peace, *whose* mind *is* stayed *on thee:* because he trusteth in thee.

⁴Trust ye in the Lord for ever: for in the Lord JEHOVAH
is everlasting strength. Isaiah 26:3-4

To love someone and to trust someone carry two distinctly different implications. People can love and have no trust, but trust cannot exist without love. Look at what Jesus said.

⁸This people draweth nigh unto me with their mouth, and honoureth me with *their* lips; but their heart is far from me. Matthew 15:8

People all over the earth, Christians included, exhibit this "moral diplomacy" in their everyday relationships with spouses, family members, friends, even God Himself. It is difficult to regain a love. To operate once again in a realm of trust is to find oneself in a gruesome struggle that seems to identify itself with a foundation that crumbles when re-tested.

We are "falsely correct" when we think that being still means to just stop moving physically. The truth is that stillness is a product of perseverance, bringing our minds, on purpose, to that quiet clarity. It is in that calm stillness that the solution will present itself. *And just how long must I be still?* However long it takes!

How many times have you ever gone before the Lord for something, and your prayer was like a teeter-totter? Do you know what I mean? Your prayer goes up and down as your mind drifts to the list of things you must accomplish that day, what went wrong yesterday, what has to be done tomorrow and then back into actual prayer. Your mind goes up to God and back down into the muddle. In that unfocused state, how can you hear God at all? In my own experience, it is the still small voice of God that speaks, and in order for me to hear His voice my own must become still.

Most people's thoughts are louder than their vocalized words. I remember someone speaking in church one time. He shared that when he had faced this same issue in prayer, he learned a good way to deal with the distracting thoughts. He would pay attention to each thought and decide whether or not it pertained to his prayer. If it did not he would say out loud, "This has nothing to do with Jesus," and he would dismiss that thought and bring his focus back on prayer.

In order to be disciplined enough to quiet our thoughts we must remember the promise we have in God's Word that we can overcome that which tries to overcome us. If we think that the enemy will not pursue us with an onslaught of imaginations, cares, and concerns, we are unwise and ignorant of his devices.

> [4](For the weapons of our warfare *are* not carnal, but mighty through God to the pulling down of strong holds;) [5]Casting down imaginations, and every high thing that exalteth itself against the knowledge of God, and bringing into captivity every thought to the obedience of Christ: 2 Corinthians 10:4-5

It has been my experience in the warfare of the mind that the hardest "nation" to conquer is the imagination. A key device in the enemy's arsenal, meant to draw us away from the answers we need, is to flood our lives with distractions. We then succumb to those distractions (in so many ways), thus detouring from the path that would lead to the resolution needed. In this way we find ourselves focused on a falseness that we think is truth.

We have allowed the pressures of not enough time and not enough energy to choke out the very thing that we all need— human interaction.

The upcoming generations are becoming technological slaves to a continual barrage of learning that replaces human relationship with devices that seem so user-friendly. In this transition to an electronic lifestyle we are overlooking the consequences…the inevitable consequences. God, in His unsearchable wisdom, designed us to communicate with each other using that which is natural to us. By God's creative ingenuity, it was designed for intimacy—a closeness that we need in order to develop character and to display the closeness that God wants us to have with Him.

A case in point is the common fairy tale beginning *Once upon a time*. Where these words used to open the door to a children's story, they now are coming to describe how often parents actually read to their children. Reading to our young children stimulated their deepest imagination with excitement and anticipation of the next adventure that awaited them. It wasn't just in a book where the adventure took place, but it was more importantly and intimately, the adventure of growing in the reflection of their parents' attention.

In the same way we have allowed the pressures of not enough time and not enough energy to choke out the very thing that we all need–human interaction. We have allowed technology to replace the greatest advancement that mankind has been given—verbal communication and imagination.

As I have observed life around me, it has become quite apparent that we have sacrificed our ability to have an intelligent conversation. In the name of convenience we have lost our intimate ability to convey hope, love, wisdom, knowledge, and joy. Real conversation births these connecting and re-enforcing influences within our souls in ways that a text or an emoji never can. In the emptiness of our emotions we have become insensitive. We are numb to the pressure to become a technological advancement ourselves with no regard to the cost, being reckless without caution, and devoid of true fulfilling purpose.

With that being said, my children are no exception. In mindless perseverance their hands seem never to fail in holding a device of some kind. By means of stimulation through excitement, challenge, colors, etc., this high tech connection sells the endless possibilities of tapping into an outside world that promises overwhelming scenes of laughter, foolishness, fictions, fables, and tragedy.

We have been immersed so long in what we feel is "normal" that we have, at the same time, existed in what is actually less than real and what can even be called abnormal. What should be used as a mere tool—this fast-paced, digital, wireless ability—has become an alternative lifestyle. God designed us to be stimulated by the beauty of His creation, yet we have replaced the real and authentic with mere electronic stimulation. That is a great loss on our parts.

We must think about this seriously. I believe there is great value in asking ourselves, *When was the last time you decided to leave your phone at home, put down your laptop or tablet, and went to a place to behold God's grace?* That's a great exercise, by the way! I encourage you to try it!

What we think is a convenience in our own lives has actually become an inconvenience. It takes away from an ever-so-present answer to problems and pressures that we battle daily. It overrides the still small voice within us, erasing the truth that God is always present with us to help in our time of need.

I challenge you; instead of picking up your phone or other device of choice, pick up instead your ability to see what happens when we behold the true beauty of God's creation. Whether it is taking the time to gaze upon a sunset over the distant horizon, or watching the rays of the sun pierce through the clouds, or standing with your feet in the caressing sand, or taking a walk on the wooded trail, there is a simple truth to be discovered. The glory of God can be seen everywhere you choose to look. Isaiah 6:3 declares the whole earth is full of His glory. His presence is right there. When you experience His glory, then clarity and stillness come.

The Certainty of Uncertainty

What am I going to do? This is our common response to pressures and problems that continually plague our day-to-day life. Pressures and problems are going to come, that's a certainty. You can count on it. When these difficult times and situations are faced calmly with faith, trust, and patient perseverance, the solutions come. Oftentimes the solutions are simple and God reveals to us a clear pathway through and out of the problems. It is when we walk mindlessly that we are blinded to this truth. In that numb state, we become infected with doubt, fear, and unbelief. We fail to realize that the enemy has launched a smokescreen over us to hide God's simple truth.

> [38]And he arose out of the synagogue, and entered into Simon's house. And Simon's wife's mother was taken with a great fever; and they besought him for her.
> [39]And he stood over her, and rebuked the fever; and it left her: and immediately she arose and ministered unto them.
> Luke 4:38-39

Most of us read this and overlook the statement of Jesus rebuking a fever because we don't realize that the problem was not actually the fever. When a person experiences a fever we get concerned about fighting the fever. We forget that the problem lies in what is causing the fever, not the fever itself.

A fever is caused by an infection—an invasion. The body is fighting an enemy, something that does not belong there. A fever is actually a defense mechanism that God has installed within us to combat infection. Every degree the body's temperature rises raises the metabolism by 10%. What is truly dangerous is a continuing high fever. This will cause proteins in the body to denature (think of the white part of an egg

The problem that exists within most people is not a virus or bacterial infection, but an "infection" of the mind, disabling them from functioning in thought as they should.

being cooked). This process unchecked will cause death eventually. This infection or intruder causes the body to not be able to function properly. This is what we clearly see in Peter's mother-in-law in this scripture because, after she was healed, she resumed her normal duty of service.

The problem that exists within most people is not a virus or bacterial infection, but an "infection" of the mind, disabling them from functioning in thought as they should. The invader or infection is often thoughts and imaginations of confusion, turmoil, fear, doubt, and disbelief, to name but a few. In the often frantic soup of these thoughts comes the additional pressure produced by the two words *what if.* Those two words are always followed by the worst scenarios our tortured minds can frame. But we must learn to stop this madness and ask ourselves this question: What are the possibilities if we would just be still and know that God is God?

> [38]Now it came to pass, as they went, that he entered a certain village: and a certain woman named Martha received him into her house.
> [39]And she had a sister called Mary, which also sat at Jesus' feet, and heard his word.
> [40]But Martha was cumbered about much serving, and came to him, and said, Lord, dost thou not care that my sister hath left me to serve alone? bid her therefore that she help me.
> [41]And Jesus answered and said unto her, Martha, Martha, thou art careful and troubled about many things:
> [42]But one thing is needful: and Mary hath chosen that good part, which shall not be taken away from her.
> Luke 10:38-42

What was the good part that Mary had chosen? Simply, she chose to be still and obediently listen to the Word of God. Christians, especially those in ministry, too often make the mistake of thinking that, being extra busy with service, we are somehow benefiting ourselves and others. But by sacrificing what is needful (to be still and know God's perfect will) we are rather bringing a detrimental effect. One word from the Master can change our whole perspective in thought and action, thus creating within ourselves priceless thoughts of peace, direction, and protection. To be able to actually hear what God is saying will always speak louder and accomplish more than what we think on our own without His input.

Surely it can't really be that simple to just be still and tell myself that God has it handled for me...can it? It is true that we have to believe that. We know it is possible to tell ourselves that truth all day long, but if we don't actually believe it, then we are just wasting our time and our words. Because we don't always have a clear understanding of this, our minds take us through a predictable series of thoughts.

It will begin with *There has to be more to it than that. I've got to figure out how I'm going to get through this. I have to weigh out all the options....* On and on these thoughts take us further and further away from allowing God to help us. By now we are busy calculating and determining what exactly we can do ourselves to bring resolution. The problem with all this calculating and weighing is that there are too many I's.

Do you know what an illusion is? Well, of course you do! You see magicians perform them all the time. They can arouse the deepest curiosity as we wonder how they were able to do the unimaginable. However, when the trick is exposed and we learn how it's done, the excitement and that captivating "something" deteriorate into nothing.

In the same way we have seen these carnal illusions materialize in an atmosphere of perplexity wrapped in a realm of seduction, awe, and wonder. These acts truly portray the master of illusion himself, Satan. His methods of madness draw millions into a mental state of encumbrance. Through his clever deceptions he envelopes them in a seduction designed to bring them to the lowest point of hopelessness. In that state, his aim is for them to draw every breath with anxiety, fear, and pain.

We must think about our own lives. Are there times when we have succumbed to the thoughts and illusions of our common enemy? It has often been the meditation of my own heart that the Word of my God not ever depart. When my thoughts begin to stray away, I begin to meditate and pray that God's thoughts would have their way in my mind.

> [8]For my thoughts *are* not your thoughts, either *are* your ways my ways, saith the Lord.
> [9]For *as* the heavens are higher than the earth, so are my ways higher than your ways, and my thoughts than your thoughts. Isaiah 55:8-9
>
> [17]How precious also are thy thoughts unto me, O God! how great is the sum of them!
> [18]*If* I should count them, they are more in number than the sand: when I awake, I am still with thee. Psalm 139:17-18

It was with the great price of Jesus' precious blood that we were bought. It was in order for us to ride with Him upon the wings of the wind, high above the storms, far above the clouds of delusion, propelled through the thunders of confusion. It is imperative that we grasp with clarity the revelation of who we are in Him and what it means for Him to be in us. Why? Because those staged moments of illusion set up by Satan are nothing more than a garish mirage of his own mockery.

What is it that makes us free? Is it not Truth? Look at what Jesus said in John 14:6 and John 8:32, "I am the way, the truth, and the life. And ye shall know the truth, and the truth shall make you free." Truth exposes lies for what they really are. Truth can expose us to a dimension of freedom that only exists within Him.

To hear Truth
Is to hear His Voice.
To hear His love
Will cause you to rejoice.
To hear Him call
Is to hear Him speak,
For His Truth will give you strength
When you are weak.

To hear His Word
Must be your desire,
For to trust in Him
Will take you higher.
Leave all of your cares behind,
And let His Peace flood your heart and mind.

The next time we find ourselves pacing the floors in our mind, wondering what to do, we must learn to just say, "Stop! Mind, be still and know that Jesus is God over this situation. I have the mind of Christ. Father, in the name of Jesus, I acknowledge You in this situation. I know You will direct my paths."

Hocus Focus

We must ask ourselves this question: Where is my focus? It is so important that we become aware of what we are looking at. During storms of confusion, doubt, pressure, and fear we must know where our focus is. Are we zeroing in on the problem or are we looking toward the solution? It can be easy to focus more on the problem than on trusting God for the answer. When the pressure is on, the problem virtually always seems bigger than the solution.

Something the Lord shared with my spirit one time was this simple revelation:

> Keep your eyes on Me
> For what you see, your heart will follow.
> To see the wrong things, in turn,
> Will leave you empty and hollow.
> This is the plan of your enemy.

As God gently holds us with His Word of faith, the enemy squeezes us with the pressure of his fear. The characteristics of God and Satan are polar opposites. Fear is faith perverted. Faith is fear converted. Whether or not we recognize it, people in every realm are operating in faith. Yes, the Christian and non-Christian alike. We all operate in faith. The determining factor comes down to what specifically we are believing in or focusing on: the power of something to hurt us or the power of the Word of God to protect and deliver us.

In the incident of Peter stepping out of the boat on a stormy sea to walk on the water to Jesus, we learn some interesting things that still apply to us today. (Read the whole story in Matthew 14:22-33.) In the end, we come to realize that Peter had more faith in the spirit of fear than he had in the faith of the Master's word that was calling him to come near. What actually caused Peter to sink were the thoughts he began to think. Once he stepped over the side of the boat and began to look around at the wind and waves, things changed. Suddenly, it didn't seem to him that Jesus was truly who He said He was.

This whole scenario was birthed from a question of doubt on Peter's part. He said, "Lord, if it is you, bid me to come." Peter's comment was actually presenting a test to Jesus. What Peter was saying was, "Jesus, prove Yourself to me, prove this faith to me." The first step Peter took on the water proved to him that this was, in fact, God. The next step—this is God—and the next step—this is God. But as he saw that which was to the left and to the right, his steps each became thoughts of *Maybe this is not really God.* By losing his focus on the answer, the pressure to fear overcame his faith in the Master's promise that he could make it.

So often we do the very same as Peter did. We say, "Lord, I thought I could do this, but I can't." We have succeeded in allowing the opportunity of our enemy to have place in our lives—right where it does not belong!

So many times in my life I experience the prompting of the Holy Spirit telling me to be still and I don't do it. There is one undeniable characteristic we all have: we tend to talk and think way too much. Let's look at a commandment we find in James 1:19.

> Wherefore, my beloved brethren, let every man be swift
> to hear, slow to speak, slow to wrath:

But we all too often find ourselves reflecting the exact opposite. We are too quick to speak and too slow to hear. In our mental marathon to resolve undesired issues on our own, we openly talk to ourselves and then engage others in hopes of finding a solution. We continuously speak the problem instead of just thanking God in faith for the answer.

Many Christians today will often use prayer as a last resort. Why is it that we will first go to everyone else, do everything and anything, but not go directly to the King? Do you remember the nursery rhyme of *Humpty Dumpty?*

Humpty Dumpty sat on a wall,
Humpty Dumpty had a great fall;
All the king's horses and all the king's men
Couldn't put Humpty together again.

Did you ever stop and wonder why they just didn't go to the king himself? We as Christians serve the greatest King (Jesus) who has ever lived and Who is more than capable of fixing the broken pieces of our shattered lives. Jesus plainly told us in Hebrews 4:16 that we are to come before the throne of grace to find help in the time of need. Our Heavenly Father wants more than anything for His children to come and pray—not to murmur and complain, but to declare to Him our situations.

> I poured out my complaint before him; I shewed before him my trouble. Psalm 142:2

The sad part is the fact that this is as far as most Christians ever get. Then they leave the throne room before ever hearing the Voice of Wisdom speak the answers that they need. In any conversation there is one simple fact that will always benefit the hearer. *What is that,* you ask? It is this. **He who knows the most needs to do the most talking.** There will always be an excuse to speak, an imagination to conquer, a distraction to ignore, a feeling to crucify. But unless you quiet yourself and be still long enough to actually hear, you may find yourself face-to-face with fear without an answer in sight.

We cannot entangle ourselves in the enemy's ploy to take us out of the realm of faith. How is it that we find ourselves in a reasoning match with our adversary whose only desire is to steal, kill, and destroy? Jesus never reasoned with Satan. He never discussed the matters that were at hand. It was always with the Word of faith that Jesus overcame His adversary.

When Satan so strategically takes the opportunity to use his scheming wiles, there is always a pressure upon us to conform to his thoughts. We often make the mistake of stepping into the ring with him, not surrounded by ropes for safety, but surrounded by a web designed to entangle our mental process. We entrap ourselves so many times in that which we thought we could understand and do on our own.

The answer is found in Romans 10:17 where we are told that Faith comes by hearing, and hearing by the word of God.

This ongoing struggle in my life has brought me ultimately to this conclusion: I will never win in a realm of reasoning with my adversary, but I will always win in a realm of faith with the Word of my God.

Many are struggling to overcome their set of current circumstances, but for them, their faith is not as strong as it once was. It is a common scene in the church world for people to stand in a prayer line and ask for increased faith in a desperate attempt to finally walk in victory.

The answer is not in praying for a faith increase. The answer is found in Romans 10:17 where we are told that *Faith comes by hearing, and hearing by the word of God.* It is so easy for us to *listen* to what is being said, and let it go in one ear and out the other. It is a whole different thing to actually listen with an intention to hear and receive what is being spoken.

A few years ago I began to find myself drawn away into a secret place where God would present Himself to me through His Word and through His creation. My experiences there would leave me tasting of the goodness (or the glory) of God in a way that would far exceed just spending time in my prayer closet. It was a place specifically created of beauty and solitude that truly outweighed man's own idea of utopia. It was as if something seemed to exude as from a canvas brushed with the warmest colors, emitting a vibrant invitation to partake.

In the midst of this place was a rocky stream of crystal clear water, echoing with its movement a peace that penetrated my soul with a longing to find its source. To follow where it went, I could easily find myself next to its flowing presence, engulfed by its voice of serenity. To my surprise, once when I was sitting next to this stream and was meditating upon the Lord, I found a question arise within my spirit: *What do you hear?* As we can all so readily do, I quickly answered, "I hear the water running." Of course, when I said that I knew it was the wrong answer.

Once again I was prompted with the question, *what do you hear?* This time I was quick to hear and slow to speak. After a few moments of stillness I replied, "I hear life." Peace then eased my mind and allowed me to know that what was spoken was a great truth. My first response to the question was the obvious answer. The second answer came from that still quiet place. This brought me to the conclusion that truth is not what I *think*, but it is what the Holy Spirit *knows*.

It is an under-estimate that as modern day Christians
we are poorly equipped
To handle the pressures that so often come our way.
Against the waves we continue to toil and row,
And that which is contrary
seems to keep us from getting to where we need to go.
We are out of strength.
We are out of longsuffering.
We are out of peace.
We are out of joy.
We are out of temperance.
We are out of meekness.
We are out of gentleness.
We are out of kindness and goodness.
We are definitely running empty without love.
We are running on fumes of faith.
In order to be equipped for this modern day
We must draw ourselves away.
Jesus will never force us to get alone to pray,
But in order to be equipped,
This truly is the only way.

Punctured

How many sermons, lesson plans, devotional quotes, Sunday school teachings, seminars, books, tapes, CDs, DVDs, websites—and last, but not least—radio broadcasts have we heard on the subject of faith? Wouldn't it seem logical that with so much training and information available, we would have received the necessary means of operating in faith the way God expects us to operate? Well, apparently we are missing something!

The increase of those who are exiting the precepts and concepts of religious faith has drastically risen, especially in the last few years. More and more pastors are quitting churches due to the pressures of having to constantly lead congregations on an "empty tank." Having continued on in despondency, they are left with a void that, regretfully, is more costly to them than what it is worth. For some it goes beyond just quitting the church. Many have chosen to give up the faith altogether. That is the most difficult decision that anyone could ever make, especially for someone who has been involved in ministry.

What astounds me is the fact that our younger generation are navigating in an opposite direction from their Christian upbringing in so many cases. The increase of our teenagers choosing not to be engaged in any kind of Christian faith should be a warning sign to those of us who proclaim to be Christ-like. We must awaken to the reality that our young warriors are lying wounded on a spiritual battleground that shows no mercy from our common adversary, Satan.

A shallow experience of Christianity gives place to the reason why so many young people, as well as others, are departing from churches. Church has been described by many as mundane, repetitious, spiritless, stale, tiring, and just plain dead. I want you to think about this statement:

How many times does your church go through the same routine Sunday after Sunday?

At what cost will the modern-day church sacrifice the power of Calvary's Cross?

They do three or four songs, make some announcements, preach or teach a word, then everyone goes home, right? I have been to churches where they do just that. In fact, I can already predict the order of events that is going to transpire next Sunday and the Sunday after that and the Sunday after that! Why is it that men and women won't step aside and allow Yahuweh to have His Way?

Another observation that is widely stated is the fact that the Bible is not being communicated in such a way that those who hear it can actually understand it. As Jesus said in Matthew 13:19, "When any one heareth the word of the kingdom, and understandeth *it* not, then cometh the wicked *one*, and catcheth away that which was sown in his heart. This is he which received seed by the way side."

All in all, I believe it can honestly be said that God seems to be unaccounted for in our "sense" of church. At what cost will the modern-day church sacrifice the power of Calvary's Cross?

There are many disturbing accounts of men and women who were once faithfully serving God, but who are now outspoken atheists. One example is of a young man who lost his faith after several years of being a Pentecostal preacher. He is now holding secular services for those who have felt the same way that he has. Another young man preached the Word of God and inspired many by being a very talented musician. He is now helping to lead a foundation through which he inspires many who are "free" thinkers or atheists like him. Once faithful ministers are now finding comfort and relief in another group that is devoted to helping ministers who have lost their faith.

These are but a tiny sampling of the many, many stories happening every day in this country as people who aren't just believers, but leaders in their various faith communities, are losing their faith and turning to secular humanism to find the answers to life's big questions.

Now that atheists are organizing and making their presence known more than ever before, the ranks of religious leaders who no longer believe and want to come out is only likely to keep growing. The questions that seem haunting to me are:

- How do ministers like these two men come to a point where they no longer believe in God?
- Why are so many people becoming disconnected from God?
- How is it that people can afford not to believe anymore?
- When will people come to the realization that God is not giving up on them, but they are giving up on Him?
- What will it take to realize there is more at stake than what we have thought?

The pressure to quit is greater than the desire to begin. Why? Because today we are seeing more and more the constant attack of one's faith from media, social arenas, economic status quos, and the world system of hierarchy (not of needs, but of wants, prestige, fortune, fame, and temporary glory).

The outside pressure to conform has seemingly triumphed over the executive internal desire to be transformed. The consequences of this only lead one into a process of being labeled as emotionally dangerous. With "true" life exhausted, one is exasperated to the point of no longer being in control. That which could have been released has now become a barricade holding everything inside. A sense of helplessness arises to enslave the mind with turmoil and weighty pressure that only seem to grow with every attempt at a liberated thought.

When one can make a statement that God seems unaccounted for in our "sense of church" we can surely realize that this is the exact opposite of the good, acceptable, and perfect will of God. How do we know this?

> For the eyes of the Lord run to and fro throughout the whole earth, to shew himself strong in the behalf of *them* whose heart *is* perfect toward him. 2 Chronicles 16:9

> But without faith *it is* impossible to please him: for he that cometh to God must believe that he is, and *that* he is a rewarder of them that diligently seek him. Hebrews 11:6

It is quite evident that God's will for His own people is to demonstrate His glory to us. We must believe that He is, that He is God, and that He is real. And we must believe that He rewards any and all who seek Him seriously and in earnest. That's the part we are responsible for. The rewarding is His part!

Church-goers all over this nation have stopped expecting when going to church.

Christians are hungry and thirsty for an outpouring of the glory of God. His glory is His goodness manifested, and with great dynamic power it fulfills the needs in the lives of His people. God is not withholding anything from us. In fact, He has given us everything He has. It is a lie of our adversary that has caused our vision to die, the same lie that Satan used in the Garden of Eden. He attempts to make us think that God is holding something back when, in actuality, God has already loosed it unto us. We are in some way longing for a change in our lives, a change from the everyday routine. We know deep down inside there are greater things to be done and wonderful things to be seen.

Church is becoming something of the natural sort. I call it a "coffee house" of the world, a place where people go and are "entertained" with good music, an inspiring word, and of course, leave a "tip" in the jar. This same process repeats over and over, while at the same time people desperately desire change in their lives.

What I clearly see is the fact that when going into churches, the hollow, shallow experiencing of God is truly leaving souls empty. But people of all ages are longing for an outpouring of Heaven's rain in a dry and thirsty land. Is it God's fault that we do not experience the fullness of Who He is? Of course not! Men and women have overstepped their bounds to the point of quenching the Holy Spirit. As a result, many are coming to church, but only going through a "routine" that leaves them just as empty as when they came in the door. Church-goers all over this nation have stopped expecting when going to church. What they may have once felt and experienced has been replaced with legalistic, political, and theoretical discussions that in no way strengthen the foundation of their faith.

It is imperative that we as a chosen people of God reflect Who He is so that others may see Who He is. As long as we continue to play church as some sort of game, things will remain the same. There is a place where the glory of Heaven collides with Earth, where the "eyes of the blind" and God's people together behold Him Who is of endless worth. In order for this to happen the flesh has to step aside to let the power of the Holy Spirit abide.

God told Jeremiah to speak out His words as commanded. In this trying time and season there is a reason for the true Word of God to be spoken: that the lies of the enemy are broken. It is a travesty that in this season of so needing God's revelation, the ministers of God are committing treason against Him. How? By operating in disobedience and by speaking their own words instead of His. The statement that the Bible is not being taught clearly or often enough is truly the evidence of the lack of God's people experiencing His glory.

Check the Oil

The pressures of this world are clearly choking the life out of our true purpose as Christians. It is in ignorance that we allow this unfortunate event to take place in our lives. We must take the time to realize the commonality that exists between engines and Christians. They both require air. They both require water and fuel. They can both suffer burnout. They both are designed with purpose. They both require maintenance. And they both require an oil of some sort.

I was taking on the task one day of mowing my yard. I have been taught that before beginning anything with machinery, always check the oil. As I checked the oil I noticed that it was significantly low. I contemplated whether or not to proceed with the mowing without adding oil because I didn't have any extra with me at the time. After tossing the question around in my mind for a time, I came to the decision that I wasn't going to run the mower with it being low on oil. As soon as I said that, the Lord was teaching me the same principle for my own life: Do not operate yourself while low on oil!

When a car's engine runs out of oil, the first thing we might notice is that the engine will not run as smoothly as it normally does. It may begin shuddering at idle when at a stoplight. Sometimes a rattling noise will be coming from under the hood. It is so important to ensure that the oil level is in normal range for a vehicle because the oil lubricates the engine. It keeps it moving. If the oil is allowed to run dry, the engine can literally seize up. This means the car will not run at all. It may end up

It is of great importance that we excel at walking in all three so we can daily experience liberty.

having to be towed to a mechanic or hauled off for salvage. Without proper oil levels, there is the possibility that the heads could crack, a head gasket can blow, a rod can be thrown through the crankcase, scoring (scuffing) can take place on the cylinder heads. This horrific and expensive list can happen to a car's engine with little or no oil. My suggestion and God's recommendation for us is this: If an engine (or we ourselves) has been running on low oil levels or without any oil for some time, it is in our best interest to add some immediately!

There are three basic provisions in the Bible—the corn, the wine, and the oil. They are also known as the Word of God, the Blood of Jesus, and the Holy Spirit. These three work in unison because they are one. It is of great importance that we excel at walking in all three so we can daily experience liberty.

Just as we must add oil to our machines so they can continue to help us accomplish what is needed, we have the same God-instituted requirements for ourselves. In Ephesians 5:18 we see the following: *And be not drunk with wine, wherein is excess; but be filled with the Spirit.* This is a command, not just a suggestion.

Being filled with the Holy Spirit, however, is not a once-and-for-all experience. There are many fillings. In the original Greek language of the New Testament the meaning of this command is clearer than what is found in most English translations. This command of God means *to be constantly and continually filled, controlled, and empowered with the Holy Spirit as a way of life.* Without Him in us to the fullest, we will suffer the same fate as a motor without oil.

Listen very carefully to the words of the Master in John 6:63:

> [63]It is the spirit that quickeneth; the flesh profiteth nothing: the words that I speak unto you, *they* are spirit, and *they* are life.

It is the oil of the Holy Spirit that allows us to operate in a fully functioning manner. It helps us accomplish what God has designed us to accomplish for His Kingdom.

> ¹And he said unto me, Son of man, stand upon thy feet, and I will speak unto thee.
> ²And the spirit entered into me when he spake unto me, and set me upon my feet, that I heard him that spake unto me. Ezekiel 2:1-2

When Ezekiel said that the *spirit* entered into him, he was saying that strength was entering into him. Power entered into him. When the oil enters in it equips.

The problem that exists within so many of us Christians is that we are never in a position long enough to hear what the Spirit has to say. Oh we are quick to say that we pray, but the question begs to be asked, "When you pray who does most of the talking?" Prayer is a two-way communication process. It is ordained by God among His people. It is meant to maintain fellowship, give and take direction, provide protection and correction. With so many pressures compounded upon us, we have allowed ourselves so little time for awareness of God, let alone time to receive the *life* that God has for us. Again it is worth saying, "He who knows the most needs to do the most talking."

With that being said, it is easier to understand those times in our lives when the Word of God doesn't seem to work, doesn't seem to produce the results we seek. Although we know that adding blue and yellow produces green, we also know that the Word of God is not a formula like that. When it is quoted and stood upon in faith, it does produce what is desired, but that desired result doesn't usually manifest instantly. That is where faith and patience come into play.

I find it a bit humorous when considering a certain incident in the book of Acts. Paul was being used mightily by God in order to bring deliverance to the captives. In one instance a certain group of "religious fanatics" decided to take it upon themselves to demonstrate what they were free to do and say.

> ¹³Then certain of the vagabond Jews, exorcists, took upon them to call over them which had evil spirits the name of the Lord Jesus, saying, We adjure you by Jesus whom Paul preacheth.

[14]And there were seven sons of *one* Sceva, a Jew, *and* chief of the priests, which did so.
[15]And the evil spirit answered and said, Jesus I know, and Paul I know; but who are ye?
[16]And the man in whom the evil spirit was leaped on them, and overcame them, and prevailed against them, so that they fled out of that house naked and wounded.
Acts 19:13-16

The fact was, these men had no idea who Jesus really was (and still is, for that matter). They had no personal relationship with Him the way that Paul did. Jesus said in John 15:7, *If ye abide in me, and my words abide in you, ye shall ask what ye will, and it shall be done unto you.*

So many are frustrated at the lack of response they seem to get when what they are thinking "is right." We cannot in any way have a relationship with the things of this world pertaining to a matter, and expect the heavens and earth to move when trouble comes or a need arises. We must each choose to be either "all in" or "all out." But in spite of this truth, many of today's "church followers" are playing what I call the spiritual Hokey Pokey with one part in and the other parts out.

The fact is that many people, Christian and non-Christian alike, are falling short. How? So many know of God, but very few actually know who God is. It is such a deception to believe that it is what we know that matters the most. In all truth, it is Who we know (Jesus) that will change our circumstances.

Be Quiet!

Being a parent can be challenging! There is a common command that erupts from parents in the moments that try their patience to its limits, when the voice of that precious little child increases to a place of producing great irritability in the parent. The parent then gives an often abrupt response to the child, "Be quiet!" The effects of the command are immediate, but short lived.

Why is it that something as simple as that could be so difficult for them to do? What is really so hard about just being quiet for a short time so that a parent can continue to focus on what they are trying to do without the continual bombardment of jabber and blabber? Their constant racket only deepens our frustration and pushes us toward our breaking point.

It is in retrospect that we remember being children ourselves and doing the same thing to our parents. And it is also true that we so often do the same thing even now to our Heavenly Father. There are times when He tells us that we need to be quiet, not because we are frustrating Him, but because He knows we need to hear His voice. But so often what do we do? We just keep filling His ears with our jabber and blabber. He knows something we have yet to learn: our whining, complaining, and murmuring will not secure the answers that we seek.

In His infinite Wisdom, God has given us a simple answer for any complicated problem, no matter what it is. Every situation that presents itself in opposition to our ability to maintain peace, love, and joy can be eradicated by the promises of God. We possess

God has not changed His mind or His plan. He is still the Great I Am today.

the ability to apply the promises through obedience. Failure to do so drains our awareness of who we were before the current crisis began.

God is the God of salvation. We have limited that salvation to pertain just to the cleansing of sin, death, and infirmities. But the full truth of it goes far beyond our limited expectation of a limitless God. Whether it is financial, marital, occupational, mental, emotional, or physical it is God Who is the author and finisher of our salvation.

When God came in the flesh upon the earth, Jesus demonstrated fully God's plan of salvation. Everywhere Jesus went He brought the full manifestation of His Father's heart for the world. God has not changed His mind or His plan. He is still the Great I Am today. If we do not truly know Him how can we know He is ready to be our triumph in turmoil? Through signs, wonders, and miracles God has proven Himself over and over again. How much longer are we going to keep asking the questions, *Who is God? Where is God?* To not know the answer to these questions is to miss the most crucial element in a Christian's walk and Satan becomes free to wreak havoc in that life.

In Psalm 46:10 God puts forth such a simple command: *Be still and know that I am God.* Isn't it something that the same words He spoke to Moses—I Am that I Am—are still as true today as when first spoken! David makes a declaration in many of the psalms ascribing Who God is unto him. David had a personal relationship with God that gave him the right to decree Who God was in his time of trouble.

> O God, thou *art* my God; early will I seek thee: my soul thirsteth for thee in a dry and thirsty land, where no water is; Psalm 63:1

Whether God was his deliverer, strong tower, healer, fortress, or provider, David understood the full spectrum of the *I Am.* It is a spiritual law that whomever we decree God to be gives Him that legal right to be just that in our lives. We must be the ones to put forth the labor of faith to know Him in His fullness, in His caring for everything about us.

In our walk of faith we must be sure to undergird that faith with patience. When the pressure is on, patience will hold up your faith. Picture, if you will, a bridge. If a military tank goes across the bridge it will succeed only if the bridge (faith) is built correctly. The pillars (patience) beneath must be strong and secure, holding the bridge steady as the tank crosses. The bridge may get a bit rocky in places, driving may slow at times. But if everything works together correctly, the tank will reach its goal.

Mind Craft

I have come to find that the greatest warfare takes place in the battle-field of the mind. Indeed, the battle won or lost there can literally be the difference between life and death. How is it that this arena of war can carry such an ultimate price? Quite simply, our thoughts are extremely important.

I have experienced for myself the consequences of an unfortified thought process that led to perpetual distress and unrest. To say, *it's just a thought; it's no big deal*, displays an ignorance of the surety of the blessing or cursing a thought can carry. As we should already know, the Kingdom of God is love, joy, and peace in the Holy Spirit. Nothing can rob that faster than a wrong thought. The power of a seemingly "no big deal" thought, depending on what it is, can raise or lower the thinker's blood pressure. It can cause laughter, tears, sadness, depression, oppression, physical sickness, and a whole range of other things. It is a mistake to imply that *it's just a thought*.

The enemy's attacks on the mind are at a staggering all-time high. More and more people are being prescribed mind-altering medications. We are seeing the effects of these pill-dependent people who live in a mental prison with no perceived way out. When the thought process is interrupted the course of life is interrupted, whether it is from a bad thought to a good thought or vice versa. Everything we do begins with a thought. God was already thinking of us before He created us. Thus with the power of the mind comes the responsibility of securing it.

I recall a time when I was in a place of mental torment after a confron-tation with someone I cared about deeply. Throughout the confronta-tion I remained calm, collected, and professional. But I allowed the things I heard in the confrontation to cause me to fall into a state of mental despair.

I had developed the habit of lying down sometimes and listening to the sounds of rain or the ocean to help me relax. After this confrontation I put on my headphones and began to listen to a thunderstorm. As soon as I began to hear the sounds of the storm, I could hear in my spirit: *Stay in the ark. No matter what you hear, feel, or see, stay in the ark.*

Soon after that experience I began to think about and meditate upon the ark—Noah's, Moses', and the Ark of the Covenant (which represents Jesus). The question I was asking was, *What are they for?* We would quickly say they were to save lives, and that is correct. But I knew there was a deeper revelation.

What came to me was that the ark specifically kept those associated with it from drowning. Noah's ark was to keep all those inside from drowning. Moses was placed in an ark (basket) to keep him from drowning. In Joshua's case, the Ark was used during the flood of the Jordan to go across so the people wouldn't drown.

When I was thinking about this the Holy Spirit brought something to my attention that was profound in the dynamics of the ark's application, that is: Anywhere there is a flood, there is a risk of drowning. When Jesus was telling me to stay in the ark, it was to keep me from drowning from the thoughts that had come against me. Just as in the occurrence of today's many catastrophic floods where people are so often caught unaware, unprepared and they drown, wrong thoughts can have the very same consequences.

God said something to us that is quite pertinent to our lives today. Look at Isaiah 59:19.

> ...When the enemy shall come in like a flood, the spirit
> of the Lord shall lift up a standard against him.

Being inquisitive about the term *standard*, I had to look it up. The word *standard* means *something considered by an authority; rule, principal or means of judgment; flag or other conspicuous object to serve as a rallying point for a military force.*

The Bible attributes many names to God because God cannot be just limited to one specific name. For instance, the revelation of His name as Jehovah Nissi: the Lord our Banner, is referring to God in the realm of warfare. God is more than willing to wage warfare on our behalf. In Exodus 15:3 we can actually see the following characteristic of God: *The Lord* is *a man of war: the Lord is his name.* When we as Christians are engaged in warfare, declaring the name of Jehovah Nissi in the midst of the situation would be to our advantage. We must remember that God's ultimate authority prevails as a force against Satan and his army.

> ³For though we walk in the flesh, we do not war after the flesh:
> ⁴(For the weapons of our warfare *are* not carnal, but mighty through God to the pulling down of strong holds;)
> ⁵Casting down imaginations, and every high thing that exalteth itself against the knowledge of God, and bringing into captivity every thought to the obedience of Christ; 2 Corinthians 10:3-5

Thoughts and imaginations are the objects of spiritual warfare where the influences of the enemy can wreak havoc on our minds. This in turn can give way to destructive actions. The ultimate goal of Satan is to wear us down until we give in and do it. He oppresses (pressures) until we give in. His constant nagging thought strategy is *Do it! Do it! Just do it! C'mon! Do it!* And all the while his temptations, thoughts, feelings, and suggestions push and pressure us to succumb to carnal desire.

The greatest accomplishment of Satan is in getting us to fight each other because it takes us away from the true source of the problem, which I am going to put into a bold statement. If the body of Christ, along with husbands and wives, would come to their senses and realize that flesh is not the enemy, but would turn on the devil, then things would change quickly!

It is of great truth that we don't wrestle against flesh and blood as Ephesians 6:12 declares. This is why the armor of God is so vital for the Christian's everyday preparation in getting dressed. The armor is the Christian's way of pushing back and pressing the enemy. Every piece of the armor of God is attached to the truth, and if we are not equipped with truth then we cannot be protected from the enemy's lies.

> [12]For we wrestle not against flesh and blood, but against principalities, against powers, against the rulers of the darkness of this world, against spiritual wickedness in high *places*.
> [13]Wherefore take unto you the whole armour of God, that ye may be able to withstand in the evil day, and have done all, to stand.
> [14]Stand therefore, having your loins girt about with truth, and having on the breastplate of righteousness;
> [15]And your feet shod with the preparation of the gospel of peace;
> [16]Above all, taking the shield of faith, wherewith ye shall be able to quench all the fiery darts of the wicked.
> [17]And take the helmet of salvation, and the sword of the Spirit, which is the word of God:
> [18]Praying always with all prayer and supplication in the Spirit, and watching thereunto with all perseverance and supplication for all saints;
> Ephesians 6:12-18
> [8]He that committeth sin is of the devil; for the devil sinneth from the beginning. For this purpose the Son of God was manifested, that he might destroy the works of the devil. 1 John 3:8

Jesus was and is the devil's undoing. This is why it is imperative for us to abide in Him and allow His words to abide in us. We must be confident of who we are in Christ and in what we can do through Him and Him alone. When people who were demon possessed came before Jesus they (the unclean spirits in them) would fall to the ground. Why? They knew Who Jesus was, and they knew their rightful place when He was present.

This has not changed one iota since then. This is why it is crucial for us to have the continual presence of God dwelling on the inside. When darkness attempts to come against us it will instead have to flee because in us should remain the light of God's glory. Darkness can only prevail in the absence of light.

With these thoughts in mind I prepared and preached a message called *Mind Craft*. The word *craft* means *skill or ability for bad purposes; cunning, deceit, guile.* With that knowledge in mind, when we see the term *witchcraft* we can associate this meaning to its purpose. We can clearly see from this definition, that Satan has his name written all over it.

We know from experiences in battles why Satan focuses on attacking the mind. If he can successfully launch an all-out attack on the mind, he can destroy the body, soul, and spirit. Satan's primary goal is to steal, kill, and destroy everything you are and sift you as wheat.

Pressures come and lead to overwhelming stress. These pressures are influenced by thoughts of overload. This causes a breakdown of our cognitive processes. And this causes many people to have nervous breakdowns, anxiety attacks, manic episodes, etc. So we can easily see why, when Satan attacks the mind, he does attack the whole person.

When Jesus was experiencing the wilderness Satan was trying to infiltrate His thought process by coming to Him in His time of weakness. The enemy loves to attack when we are hurt, angry, lonely, or tired. That is when we are the most vulnerable. We have all reached the place where we just start saying things out of anger toward God. It happens when you're tired, frustrated, and just want to quit. Right?

Who do you think is manipulating the scene at that point? What you were saying was a reflection of the <u>thoughts</u> that were in your mind. Now Satan can't make us say anything we don't want to say. Still, his strategy is to plant those thoughts, trying to get you to speak death.

> [20]A man's belly shall be satisfied with the fruit of his mouth; *and* with the increase of his lips shall he be filled. [21]Death and life *are* in the power of the tongue: and they that love it shall eat the fruit thereof. Proverbs 18:20-21

The devil knows this scripture! We must know it, too, and act on it! But how? The only way to fight the enemy in the realm of this kind of warfare is with faith-filled anointed words. We are not fighting a physical war which so many Christians are giving place to today. In Paul's words they are *beating the air*. They are screaming, yelling, and waving all around, but after it is all said and done, they are just tired, and have accomplished nothing. Christians all over the world are what I would call "loading their guns" and not loading their mouths with anointed words.

How does Jesus fight? The Word of God tells us exactly!

> ¹⁶And he had in his right hand seven stars: and out of his mouth went a sharp two-edged sword: and his countenance *was* as the sun shineth in his strength. Revelation 1:16

> ¹⁶Repent; or else I will come unto thee quickly, and will fight against them with the sword of my mouth. Revelation 2:16

This is why it is so vital to have the Holy Spirit's help in combating the spiritual realm so we can do it by God's Word of faith. When the Master speaks we know that circumstances change. We, as the army of God, must have divine direction in order to experience divine victory. It cannot and will not come naturally. When His Word is nigh, then victory is nigh.

> ⁸But what saith it? The word is nigh thee, *even* in thy mouth, and in thy heart: that is, the word of faith, which we preach; Romans 10:8

> ¹¹So shall my word be that goeth forth out of my mouth: it shall not return unto me void, but it shall accomplish that which I please, and it shall prosper *in the thing* whereto I sent it. Isaiah 55:11

Truth is always simple and easy to entreat. If we hold onto truth and be a doer of the Word of God, then we cannot suffer defeat.

[10]For thus saith the Lord, That after seventy years be accomplished at Babylon I will visit you, and perform my good word toward you, in causing you to return to this place.

[11]For I know the thoughts that I think toward you, saith the Lord, thoughts of peace, and not of evil, to give you an expected end. Jeremiah 29:10-11

These verses give us a clear understanding of God's thoughts toward us. Anything that is contrary to this cannot be the will of God. God says to us directly, "I know the thoughts that I think toward you." The big question is, *do we know the thoughts that God thinks toward us?*

In verse 10 we see a reference to Babylon. Any time we see that word used, it is associated with captivity. It is not a place that God desires His children to experience. However, because of the choices we make and the thoughts we think, we, too, often end up there. That's why, when God says that He would perform His good word toward us in causing us to return to this place, He is referring to bringing us back to where we belong—in our rightful place.

It is simple and invaluable to always remember that God thinks peace and good toward us; Satan always thinks evil and confusion. For each thought that comes to us we must ask ourselves the question: *Where does this thought take me, low or high?* If they are bringing us down they are of Satan; if they take us higher they are of God. In Isaiah 55:9 God simply states that His thoughts are higher than our thoughts, His ways are higher than ours. Therefore it follows that thoughts from God will take us higher; thoughts from Satan will always take us down.

It follows that thoughts from God will take us higher; thoughts from Satan will always take us down.

Have you noticed how we even talk this truth without realizing it? We say someone is *down* when they are suffering from depression, loneliness, sadness. Yes and the *down* is the result of thoughts introduced by the devil. Stay around someone who is depressed long enough, and that oppressing spirit can be felt trying to come against everyone around. I dare say that most people are not suffering from a chemical imbalance, but rather, a spiritual imbalance.

This doesn't agree with what the doctor says, but we have to realize that a spiritual condition cannot be treated with a natural solution. We must recognize that we live in a spiritual world with real demonic forces at work to destroy the knowledge of Christ Who resides within us.

Satan has no problem with medication. In fact, he's all for it because if it doesn't heal, it just makes the person numb to the root of the problem. What gives the devil trouble is when people think about Jesus because he knows the power of thought. Healing has to take place at the source, and Satan is 100% of the problem. God once told me this:

> Get out of the places that keep you low,
> And into the high place you must go!

> ³For though we walk in the flesh, we do not war after the flesh:
> ⁴(For the weapons of our warfare *are* not carnal, but mighty through God to the pulling down of strong holds;)
> ⁵Casting down imaginations, and every high thing that exalteth itself against the knowledge of God, and bringing into captivity every thought to the obedience of Christ; 2 Corinthians 10:3-5

This scripture must be heeded in order for us to be victors in this world. The absolute worse "nation" we can try to conquer is our own imagination. Everything that these verses talk about is dealing with the war that takes place in our minds. We must realize that we hear more than we think we hear. We've all had the experience of saying something only to follow it up with the thought or comment, "Why did I say that?" The reason we said that thing we immediately questioned is because a thought was planted in our minds and we responded to that thought.

So how is the thought planted? Quite easily. It comes in through what the enemy speaks. He can't be heard unless he has a willing listener and a mouthpiece. When we think about a past argument with someone we really love, instead of expressing love we spoke out words of hate, anger, frustration, or resentment. Where did those horrible words come from? They may start easy like, but then the pressure to express them increases. The point of no return finally comes and we buckle under that pressure of anger, hatred, or whatever. We release those weapons of mass destruction, words that are intended to cut and destroy that very one we love.

> For where envying and strife *is,* there *is* confusion and
> every evil work. James 3:16

We know that God is not the author of confusion. We know He does not abide in confusion. Truly we can say, *No peace, no Jesus. Know Jesus, know peace.*

A major aspect of mental salvation comes from applying the Word of God to our everyday lifestyle. To neglect this Word is to neglect abundant life. How is it then that millions today pursue an opposing path that leads to pain and strife?

> [1]The Lord is my shepherd; I shall not want.
> [2]He maketh me to lie down in green pastures: he leadeth me beside the still waters.
> [3]He restoreth my soul: he leadeth me in the paths of righteousness for his name's sake.
> [4]Yea, though I walk through the valley of the shadow of death, I will fear no evil: for thou *art* with me; thy rod and thy staff they comfort me.
> [5]Thou prepares a table before me in the presence of mine enemies: thou anointest my head with oil; my cup runneth over.
> [6]Surely goodness and mercy shall follow me all the days of my life: and I will dwell in the house of the Lord for ever. Psalm 23:1-6

This psalm reveals to us that Jesus is our Shepherd. In Him we shall not lack. It would be very wise on our part to seek the One Who promises such blessings! Where most of us fail to obtain stable mental health is in our life commitments. A commitment is just the simple act of pledging or engaging oneself, of setting priorities. So where do so many of us seem to be committed or engaged so very much? Well, it's different for each of us because we have each prioritized our personal life the way we see fit.

The Word of God has something to say about this area of our lives. Read it in Proverbs 16:3:*Commit thy works unto the Lord, and thy thoughts shall be established.*

Isn't it interesting that this verse makes the connection between our commitments and our thoughts? It's also interesting how many scriptures point to mental health. God wants us to be whole! What is God telling us here? To me, I hear Him saying that whatever we do, we had better have the Lord involved in it. If He's not, then we don't really have peace. This is what cripples and paralyzes so many among us—their works being committed unto everything but God.

> [13]I can do all things through Christ which strengtheneth
> me. Philippians 4:13

We like to quote this scripture, but many misuse it. This verse must be taken in its context. It cannot be used with success if we are trying to apply it to something that has nothing to do with God's work or plan for our lives. Paul was in the perfect will of God. And yes, he was suffering for it, but it was through Christ that he was able to continue in strength above his own. If we are outside of the will of God for our lives, then the blessing of strength cannot be there. At that point, we are limited to mercy and grace.

To put it simply, the choice is ours. We must continue to stay in the ark. When I was thinking about this, I came up with a great acronym for *ark*. It's easy to remember it this way. **A**lways **R**emain **K**ept. We are kept in the peace, love, and joy in the Holy Spirit. Outside the ark there is only that which is empty and dark.

The Distraction Infraction

One of the greatest strategies that the devil likes to use is the tool of distraction. Yes, I said tool. And he truly does know how to wield it in our lives if we will let him. The purpose of distraction is to keep us from walking the straight and narrow, to keep us from achieving the goal the Lord has intended for our lives. Distraction causes us to step off the path and miss out on what God has for us. Distractions, if not stopped, will open the door to fear, doubt, iniquity, infirmity, poverty, vanity, insanity, and calamity.

How many times has God led you to do something specific whether it was to go somewhere, or help someone, or build something, etc.? And when you started to step out and do it, the storms started to rage against you? You're probably saying *amen to that, brother!* Did you not find it "ironic" that something like that happened as soon as you were doing what the Lord wanted you to do?

It is nothing more than a distraction from the enemy to get you to either alter your course or give up altogether. What has been your reaction? Did you stay the course, alter the course, or give place to fear, doubt, and unbelief and just quit? The very same circumstance happened to Jesus and His disciples in the fourth chapter of Mark.

> [35]And the same day, when the even was come, he saith unto them, Let us pass over to the other side.
> [36]And when they had sent away the multitude, they took him even as he was in the ship. And there were also with him other little ships.
> [37]And there arose a great storm of wind, and the waves beat into the ship, so that it was now full.

³⁸And he was in the hinder part of the ship, asleep on a pillow: and they awake him, and say unto him, Master, carest thou not that we perish?
³⁹And he arose, and rebuked the wind, and said unto the sea, Peace, be still. And the wind ceased, and there was a great calm.
⁴⁰And he said unto them, Why are ye so fearful? how is it that ye have no faith? Mark 4:35-40

Jesus had a clear and direct command to go to the other side of the sea because He knew that his mission was to set a demonic man free. Except, not long after, a great storm arose—no doubt a distraction caused by the enemy. Why? To put them into a state of extreme fear, and ultimately to try to take their lives.

The distraction succeeded in doing so, for the disciples thought that was going to be the end of their lives. They questioned Jesus' very love for them at that moment, as most people do. They could have even questioned whether or not what Jesus had told them to do had really been God at all.

Do not forget that you have an adversary and when doing things contrary to him, you are in the midst of warfare. You must be ready to fully engage. Learn to discern the enemy's distractions that come in all different forms, shapes and sizes. Use your God-given authority to take charge just as Jesus did and maintain your course.

There is no way of knowing the countless times distraction has come into the church or even our own personal lives. It has caused us to miss what God was speaking through the pastor, evangelist, or minister. To truly hear what was being said is to drastically change our thought processes. (Remember Romans 10:17 that says faith comes by hearing and hearing by the word of God.)

What are distractions designed to do? To make us lose our focus.

Those thoughts then go on to change our steps, which change our direction, which changes our experience of great victory and protection.

Something that can seem insignificant as a distraction from the enemy is able to cause us to leave a church or a situation the same way we came into it.

What are distractions designed to do? To make us lose our focus. Focus on what? Our focus on Christ Himself and who we are in Him. As long as we are focused on Jesus we are steadfast. But when distraction takes us over we become infracted. The word *infracted* means *to violate; to break a law, break a promise; to transgress; to breach.*

What is it that takes away from Jesus in our lives? It can be all kinds of things such as other people, phones, problems, jobs, recreational habits, money, television, social media, and perceived needs. There are all kinds of distractions seemingly styled just for each of us, and their sole purpose is to lead us off the path the Lord has prepared for us.

When I was a youth pastor I made the comment to my youth group that one of the biggest distractions the enemy will use in your life is the opposite sex. I don't know how many lives have gone off track because of this. Remember the enemy is very sly in what he will try in order to bring someone into your life that seems just like the one you are believing and praying for.

When God told Samuel to go to Jesse's house to anoint David as the new king, God never told Samuel what David looked like. Upon arriving at Jesse's house he took a look at Eliab and said, "Surely the Lord's anointed is before me." But the Lord said unto Samuel, "Look not on his countenance, or on the height of his stature; because I have refused him: for *the Lord seeth* not as man seeth; for man looketh on the outward appearance, but the Lord looketh on the heart"(See I Samuel 16:6-7).

We often focus on the outside and never ask the Lord to help us see the heart of the person. So much suffering and pain could be avoided by just taking the time to ask God to show us instead of basing it on our own judgment.

Satan knows the power of the Word of God. He also knows how effective it is when we mix it with faith. He knows that if he can keep us from the thoughts and plans God has for us, he can hold us in captivity, our own little Babylon. This is the opposite of what God desires for every person!

Once in a quiet time with the Lord he shared something with me. He showed me: *The purpose of Peter walking on the sea was to come to see Me, but because of distraction many fail to reach their destiny.* Just how easy is it to become distracted? It is literally one thought away! Just one thought can take us away from the place where we need to be. We see something distracting and we end up giving place to the enemy. Something we hear brings fear. Something we feel can seem so real and so opposite to what God has told us. Distractions are all around, and their primary purpose is to cause us to fall to the ground...as hard as possible!

> [35] And this I speak for your own profit; not that I may cast
> a snare upon you, but for that which is comely, and that
> ye may attend upon the Lord without distraction.
> 1 Corinthians 7:35

Many Christians desire to go higher, but to do so we must give up the things that cause us to tire, to be moved away from God's plan. The choice is ours daily. Paul in this scripture made this comment after talking about being married to the opposite sex and how each one would be more concerned on pleasing the other than concentrating on the Lord. The statement in verse 35 holds true in every aspect. The word *attend* in that verse means *to minister to, assist, and pay attention to.*

It was interesting to me to see the word *assist* in the definition due to the fact that we as Christians actually can be considered "executive assistants." What is the job description of an executive assistant? They work hard to make a career of juggling tasks for higher-ups. Executive assistants may find themselves in servitude to their CEO or boss. But they may also find themselves at a proverbial and literal seat at the table on their boss's behalf.

No matter what the task at hand, the executive assistant must be prepared for anything. His or her basic responsibilities are to manage the boss's calendar, coordinate meetings, take messages, and a wide range of other duties. They are tasked with providing high level administrative support for the company and its top executives.

He knew He had been contracted by the Father, and upon that promise He enacted.

We as Christians perform the same role for the Lord throughout the body of Christ. We must ask ourselves, "Can I be effective in that job description if I am prone to distractions?" We must be prepared for anything. When Jesus walked the earth He was prepared for anything and everything. How did He do that? He didn't allow Himself to be distracted. He knew He had been contracted by the Father, and upon that promise He enacted.

Paul in this scripture said: *This I speak for your own profit.* What does profit mean? Profit refers to the financial benefit realized when the amount of revenue gained from a business activity exceeds the expenses, costs, and taxes needed to sustain the activity. Profit from that business belongs to the business owner.

Now, in what business are we as Christians supposed to be fully engaged? The Kingdom business. Only meaningful work brings true satisfaction while meaningless work brings distraction. It's worth saying again: We as Christians are to be fully engaged in God's Kingdom. And I will add that if we are not so engaged, we have become lost to the very purpose of Calvary's cross. It was on that hill a transformation came, taking us who believe from death to life, from being lost to gaining salvation. If we neglect His true purpose, we make it a desecration.

It is imperative that we make certain what we are doing involves God and that it is His good, acceptable, and perfect will for us. If not, then we continue to walk a crooked and broken path giving way to heartache, pain, suffering, and turmoil.

Blood Pressure

When it comes to our physical bodies God has designed and created them with such wisdom, knowledge, and understanding! Our bodies are very much like a machine engineered to function in a precise manner. David said it best in Psalm 139:14: *I will praise thee; for I am fearfully and wonderfully made.* Our internal and external organ systems (there are 11 of them) all work together interdependently, operating on levels that ascribe only to God the deep reverence of being who we are.

After spending two semesters in the study of anatomy and physiology, I came to a deeper realization of the marvelous design laid out by our Heavenly Father in creating us. By His design our bodies have receptors that feel pain, pressure, and temperature. Their purpose is to protect us from harm.

In fact, when it comes to touch or pressure, this is actually a form of mechanical energy. There are nearly 500,000 sensory receptors located in the skin that detect pressure. When sensory information is detected by these mechanoreceptors, it travels from the skin to the spinal cord, the brain stem, the thalamus, and finally to the somatosensory areas in the frontal and parietal lobes of the brain. Of course, this all takes place in a mere fraction of a second.

The main organ system within our bodies is the cardiovascular or circulatory system. It is composed of the heart, blood vessels, and blood which are responsible for transporting nutrients, chemical messengers, gases, and wastes. With each beat of our hearts blood is being pumped around our bodies. This enables our muscles to receive the energy and oxygen they need. For this to work properly, the heart pushes blood through the arteries into the rest of the body. The blood is then returned to the heart through another network of blood vessels called veins or the venous system.

When blood passes through the arteries it pushes against the sides of our blood vessels. The strength of that pushing is called blood pressure. When our heart compresses and forces the blood through our arteries, our blood pressure goes up. And when our heart relaxes, our pressure goes down. (Notice the benefits of relaxation: pressure is relieved.) With every heartbeat our blood pressure actually elevates to a higher level, then falls to a lower level. When you have your blood pressure checked, the nurse or doctor tells you the readings which represent the highest and lowest levels detected. This high and low are also known as systolic (highest) and diastolic (lowest) readings.

Many people in this world today suffer from hypertension, or high blood pressure. This means their maximum levels exceed the normal limits we are to have. The frightening thing about uncontrolled high blood pressure is that it can lead to a stroke. A stroke will weaken or damage the blood vessels in the brain, causing them to narrow, leak, or rupture.

Why am I talking about blood pressure? I am laying a foundation as to the effects of how pressure—not just on the inside, but coming from the outside—greatly influences physical health.

In day-to-day life we experience situations that cause us to feel pressure. We deal with burdens, traumas, depression, oppression, workloads, busy schedules, financial pressures, health issues, and so much more. So often it is a combination of these pressures that drives (pushes) us, just like the heart pushes the blood.

Everything we were depending on and trying to hold onto soon crumbles into dust.

The maximum pressures become so great that we reach a place which is the most dangerous to ourselves–our breaking point, or rupturing point. It is at this time that we succumb to the then inevitable "breakdown." The pressure becomes too great. We buckle under the weight of that pressure, and we find ourselves *crushed* to the point of having nothing left. At that time hope vanishes, peace leaves, and strength ebbs away completely. Everything we were depending on and trying to hold onto soon crumbles into dust.

We have all experienced in some way the pressures that life has to offer, and we have each dealt with them in different ways. Sometimes we have become so overwhelmed that we begin to sink into despair and frustration. In that desperation we have made mistakes that cost us more than it was really worth in the end.

No matter how bad the pressures may be in our lives, they shall never be nearly as bad as what Jesus faced that night in the garden of Gethsemane. This was the night of his betrayal by Judas. Read the dramatic story as it unfolds here:

> [36]Then cometh Jesus with them unto a place called Gethsemane, and saith unto the disciples, Sit ye here, while I go and pray yonder.
> [37]And he took with him Peter and the two sons of Zebedee, and began to be sorrowful and very heavy. Matthew 26:36-37

We can clearly see that Jesus was experiencing the pressure of what was about to befall Him. But He did the only thing that was necessary in times of heaviness. He prayed. We should do the same thing in our own lives.

I don't want to stop there because that was not the full extent of His internal pain. If we go to Luke's account of this scene we get a little deeper look.

> [44]And being in an agony he prayed more earnestly: and his sweat was as it were great drops of blood falling down to the ground. Luke 22:44

There is a medical term for this phenomenon. It is called *hematidrosis,* a very rare condition in which a human will actually sweat blood. Around our sweat glands are found multiple blood vessels. When a person is under the pressure of great stress the blood vessels constrict. When the stress wears off the blood vessels dilate to the point of rupturing and the blood flows into the sweat glands. As the sweat glands produce a lot of sweat, it pushes the blood to the surface where it comes out as droplets of blood mixed with sweat.

The fact is, Jesus was under so much pressure or weight that it produced such an effect. What was the pressure coming at Jesus that night? He knew that He would soon take on such a tremendous load of guilt for our sins at the cross. He knew the Father would have to forsake Him. And worst of all, He knew he would face hell itself for us. No matter how hard our circumstances have been in the past or are in the present moment, there is nothing that we have or will experience that can come close to what Jesus endured for us. (An interesting side note is that the meaning of Gethsemane is *press*.)

Trapped

Feeling trapped—it's a feeling and experience desired by neither man nor beast. With no perceived way out we feel the pressure of defeat. Anxiety and fear consume every possible thought of hope. We become so aware of our weaknesses, of our vulnerability. Entrapment leads us to question our intelligence. No matter how smart we think we are, when trapped we struggle with trying to escape the present circumstance, only finding that no way out exists.

When fear tries to take hold of our minds we find ourselves faced with an associated feeling, and that is *death*. Death can come in many forms and be experienced in different ways. It is not always a physical manifestation. Entrapment brings thoughts of hopelessness which point us in the mental direction of just wanting to give up. At some point we ask ourselves, *Why try? What's the point? Why me? How did this happen? What did I do wrong?*

It is a common fact that we get trapped in different areas of our lives, and yes, some situations are our own fault. But more often than not, situations arise in which our faith is greatly tested to see how we will respond to the pressure of being "trapped." We become trapped in job situations, relationships, gangs, addictions, consequences from wrong choices, and so many other things. When we find ourselves feeling trapped we always begin to look for a way out of our misery. Unfortunately, too many times it seems like the only way out is death.

The problem is that the situation causes us to become narrow minded. We develop tunnel vision

God so very much wants to demonstrate His power toward us because His very name is Salvation.

with our focus more on the problem itself instead of asking God for His solution.

Remember in the book of Exodus when the Israelites were delivered from Egypt. The Israelites came to the end of the road with no place to go. It *appeared* to them that they had the Egyptian army on one side and the Red Sea on the other side. This scenario set up the sense of being trapped, thus setting the stage for fear, doubt, confusion, and complaining.

In the midst of this pressured situation Moses spoke what the Lord still tells us today, "Fear not!" Why? Because if we will be still long enough, God will make the way out and lead us, if we'll let Him. The simple truth is that anytime we think we can, He won't. The simplest solution in our "trapped" circumstance is to acknowledge to God that, whether or not it is our fault, we are in the situation, and we cannot get out of it without His help. God so very much wants to demonstrate His power toward us because His very name is *Salvation.* He has been and always will be faithful to that characteristic of His own name.

The Israelites became so afraid because of the scenario unfolding around them that they thought they were going to die. They saw no other possible outcome. But bear in mind that their departure from Egypt was the perfect will of God. It is much easier to face adversity in the perfect will of God than outside of it. It is safer there in His will.

The key to coming through these trapped places lies in our focus. We are so aware of what looms to our left and threatens to our right, but why is it we are not looking up? Psalm 121 sheds a lot of light on this:

> [1]I will lift up mine eyes unto the hills, from whence cometh my help.
> [2]My help *cometh* from the Lord, which made heaven and earth.
> [3]He will not suffer thy foot to be moved: he that keepeth thee will not slumber.
> [4]Behold, he that keepeth Israel shall neither slumber nor sleep.

> ⁵The Lord *is* the keeper: the Lord *is* thy shade upon thy right hand.
> ⁶The sun shall not smite thee by day, nor the moon by night.
> ⁷The Lord shall preserve thee from all evil: he shall preserve thy soul.
> ⁸The Lord shall preserve thy going out and thy coming in from this time forth, and even for evermore. Psalm 121:1-8

Let's look at another example in the scriptures about feeling trapped.

> ¹⁷And it came to pass on a certain day, as he was teaching, that there were Pharisees and doctors of the law sitting by, which were come out of every town of Galilee, and Judaea, and Jerusalem: and the power of the Lord was *present* to heal them.
> ¹⁸And, behold, men brought in a bed a man which was taken with a palsy: and they sought *means* to bring him in, and to lay *him* before him.
> ¹⁹And when they could not find by what *way* they might bring him in because of the multitude, they went upon the housetop, and let him down through the tiling with *his* couch into the midst before Jesus. Luke 5:17-19

These men who brought their sick friend to Jesus to be healed walked into a situation where they must have felt a bit trapped, too. There were so many people present in the room that there was no way to get their friend and his bed close enough to the Master to gain His attention. They looked to the left and saw the multitude. They looked to the right and saw the multitude.

The Israelites looked left and saw Egyptians; they looked right and saw the Red Sea. What they saw in their own minds was that escape was an impossibility. The plan of the enemy is always to get us to think that way. He wants us to focus more on the impossible than on the God of "All Things Possible." The enemy's thoughts plague our minds with *I can't; I'm stuck; I guess it's all over; there's no way out now; I'm too far in.* Those are all lies which many of us have bought into from time to time. But if we will just heed Psalm 121 and look up, we can see God showing us the way of escape. This is the demonstration of God's mighty salvation!

Option "C"

Satan is an adversary not to be taken lightly. We must be keenly aware of his methods of operation at all times so we can overcome his wiles. I want to reveal a common strategy he uses in hopes of bringing us into that pressure of entrapment.

It's very simple, and unfortunately, quite effective against those unassuming and unaware. He likes to instigate situations for us that adamantly portray **only** two options, neither of which will bring a desirable outcome. It is a trap that Satan uses all the time to force us into making a decision based on the options he shows us—either or, left or right, this or that.

Jesus was not exempt from Satan's game either. Look at this example from the scriptures.

> [1]Jesus went to the mount of Olives.
> [2]And early in the morning he came again into the temple, and all the people came unto him; and he sat down, and taught them.
> [3]And the scribes and Pharisees brought unto him a woman taken in adultery; and when they had set her in the midst,
> [4]They say unto him, Master, this woman was taken in adultery, in the very act.
> [5]Now Moses in the law commanded us, that such should be stoned: but what sayest thou?
> [6]This they said, tempting him, that they might have to accuse him. But Jesus stooped down, and with *his* finger, wrote on the ground, *as though he heard them not.*
> John 8:1-6

I want to pause here and shed some light on what is taking place in these verses. This whole episode was a set-up (a trap) from the very beginning in order to bring accusation against Jesus. They were out to discredit His character. What the scribes and Pharisees said according to the Law of Moses was true, except there was a huge missing component to the scene.

Leviticus 20:10 shows us the missing element. *And the man that committeth adultery with* another *man's wife, even he that committeth adultery with his neighbour's wife, the adulterer and the adulteress shall surely be put to death.* This is the Law of Moses these men were bringing up to Jesus in this incident. But where was the man, the adulterer? If she was caught "in the very act" of adultery, why didn't they bring the man, too? I wonder how many people just read over this fact.

So we see that this whole set-up is a game that is played by the enemy. This plot against Jesus' character was meant to pressure Him into choosing what I like to call the option scenario. We have all had the experience of having to choose between option A and option B. In this scenario those are the only two choices we are allowed, A or B. This tactic is meant to limit our thinking to only these options.

Jesus showed us in this situation a break-away from the option game pressure. He basically said, *What about option C?* Had Jesus responded with option A He would have contradicted Moses. This would have led into His being condemned as a false prophet. Besides that, what would the people have thought if He had turned and done that? They would be thinking, *this guy isn't who we thought He was after all.* If Jesus had chosen option B the woman would have been stoned to death. That would have led to Him being accused to the Romans of usurping authority.

The pressure was on, and the scribes and Pharisees thought for sure they had Him this time.

This is a prime example of how, if we are not careful to ask God for help in times of decision making, we can end up in real trouble really fast. The pressure was on, and the scribes and

Pharisees thought for sure they had Him this time. They believed they had Him between a rock and a hard place.

Who among us has not been in that situation before! The pressure comes through thoughts that *people are waiting on you to make the decision.* And with that pressure comes that feeling of being rushed and hurried, of not having the time to be still and know that He is God. Thus we end up making a decision that causes pain and heartache.

We can also make the observation in this plot against Jesus that it was not just trying to trap the Master. The woman herself was trapped as well. Remember earlier that I mentioned that, with the feeling of being trapped, sometimes the only way out seems to be death. Well, for this woman, that was surely the case. As she stood there in the midst of this group listening to the words these men spoke with her life hanging in the balance, it must have crossed her mind that this was it. Her life must be over no matter what. When she looked to the right she saw her accusers, and to the left she saw the crowd. Escape must have looked impossible to her.

We must always remember that Satan is a liar. Anything and everything he initiates is defeated if we will only be still and know that Jesus is God. Satan tries to pressure us into thinking that the only option we have is a bad one. That is one of the greatest lies of all! In times of trouble, it is up to us to call upon Him for help in every circumstance. In the book of James we find truth that applies to this situation.

> 5If any of you lack wisdom, let him ask of God, that giveth to all *men* liberally, and upbraideth not; and it shall be given him.
> 6But let him ask in faith, nothing wavering. For he that wavereth is like a wave of the sea driven with the wind and tossed.
> 7For let not that man think that he shall receive any thing of the Lord.
> 8A double minded man *is* unstable in all his ways.
> James 1:5-8

We have to ask for wisdom in order to apply Option C which will cause us to experience the best outcome in our situation. In the scenario with this woman caught in adultery there was wisdom to be applied. Look at how Jesus foiled the devil's plan with Heavenly wisdom. It wasn't only Heavenly wisdom, but a Heavenly love. The combination caused the whole situation to diffuse.

Let's read to see what happened when Jesus chose Option C.

> [7]So when they continued asking him, he lifted up himself, and said unto them, He that is without sin among you, let him first cast a stone at her.
> [8]And again he stooped down, and wrote on the ground.
> [9]And they which heard *it,* being convicted by *their own* conscience, went out one by one, beginning at the eldest, *even* unto the last: and Jesus was left alone, and the woman standing in the midst.
> [10]When Jesus had lifted up himself, and saw none but the woman, he said unto her, Woman, where are those thine accusers? hath no man condemned thee?
> [11]She said, No man, Lord. And Jesus said unto her, Neither do I condemn thee: go, and sin no more. John 8:7-11

The response which Jesus used was in Godly wisdom. It caused the pressure to be relieved, not only in His position, but also in the woman's. The next time we feel trapped or pressured into making a decision between two seemingly "only" options, neither of which promises a desired outcome, we must stop! Rather than jumping to A or B, we must ask God for His wisdom to show us Option C and how to implement it. And through it all we must remember: *Anything over our head is under His feet!*

I Am

We've probably all heard someone say at some point, *I am not who you think I am!* Truth be known, we've probably all said it ourselves at one time. What does that statement mean? First, let's answer that question with another question: *Who do you think you are?* That's an important question for each of us to ponder and answer. How we answer that question for ourselves is quite important.

In our society today there are many people who cannot answer that question. It seems as if the only possible answer they have is what somebody else says about who they are. Pressure can obviously come in a variety of forms, wearing a host of disguises. It comes through as many different means as the devil can possibly utilize against us. By not knowing who we are ourselves we open the way for the specific pressure that comes from listening to the opinions of everyone around us.

This is easy to recognize in the realm of parenting. A child growing up can experience the pressure of what other people want them to be. Too often kids are pressured into continuing the family tradition of an occupational field that has been in the family for generations. The flip side of that is the pressure that comes to the child who is expected to break that family tradition of generations and do something completely different. In either case the child is pressured with the challenge of living up to someone else's expectations.

With this increasing conflict today concerning identity crisis, it becomes obvious that pressures are bringing more and more confusion and chaos. Let's look at the definition of identity crisis. This term is defined this way: *n. A psychosocial state or condition of disorientation and role; confusion occurring especially in adolescents as a result of conflicting pressures and expectations and often producing acute anxiety.*

Now we as Christians know that the author of confusion is none other than Satan himself. His tactics or wiles are often at work when other people in our lives try to pressure us into ignoring the truth of the Holy Spirit within us. He attempts to remove us in this way from the abundant life God intends for us.

Each of us has a destiny, a real purpose in life. That destiny is not about who we are or what we have experienced, good or bad. Our life experiences do not change the plan God has for us. The sad truth is that most of the pressure that comes toward us, attempting to move us away from that awesome destiny, comes from our families, those closest to us. It's really not so hard to understand this, though, when we take the time to think it through. There is no one in our lives that knows our hearts more than we ourselves do. Not our spouses, parents, siblings or other family members or close friends. Why is it, then, that we so often compromise our own innate desires in order to satisfy someone else's opinion—what they think we should or should not be or do?

God has planted something in each one of us that is to be developed, nurtured, and purposed for His own glory. If Satan can detour us from doing that, he can succeed in stealing precious time and precious purpose out of our lives.

Feeling obligated is a pressure that so many feel. In an attempt to not hurt that other person's feelings, an A or B decision is made to keep the peace. In these situations the only ones whose feelings are being hurt, indeed, are we ourselves.

Pressure from family affects us in so many ways. We all too often become stuck in an "expectation" rut. Those around us who have not figured out their own true purpose in life can exert a great deal of effort and influence trying to steer us in "the right direction." I speak with a degree of sarcasm here, of course, but

It is not a light thing to ignore what is in our hearts.

the truth is still there. It is not a light thing to ignore what is in our hearts. And the pressure of feeling persecuted, abandoned, ridiculed, mocked, and despised all come to play in our own minds, causing us to question the fact of our own true identities.

The only one responsible for each of our lives is us! If we allow others to influence us in ways contrary to what God has placed in our own hearts, we are defying and denying our ability to be what God has chosen for us to be.

David was intended for great purposes in the Kingdom of God. Through being a shepherd boy God was developing him for something greater— to become the king for the people of Israel. When young David was getting ready to confront the mighty Goliath he declared unto Saul the works that God had done in his life by defeating the beasts that had come to attack his flock. He had used what he knew he was good at in the fields tending and protecting the flock. After Saul heard what David had to say, he implied that he knew what David was going to need in his attempt to get the job done.

> [38] And Saul armed David with his armour, and he put an helmet of brass upon his head; also he armed him with a coat of mail.
> [39] And David girded his sword upon his armour, and he assayed to go; for he had not proved *it*. And David said unto Saul, I cannot go with these; for I have not proved *them*. And David put them off him.
> [40] And he took his staff in his hand, and chose him five smooth stones out of the brook, and put them in a shepherd's bag which he had, even in a scrip; and his sling *was* in his hand: and he drew near to the Philistine.
> 1 Samuel 17:38-40

Saul put armor on David that David was not familiar with. David put it on and tried to go out against the enemy, but the armor was not "him." It didn't feel right, and indeed, it was not needed in order to accomplish the divine task at hand. So David took all of it off and equipped himself instead with what he knew in his own heart he needed. Of course, we know that he succeeded; Goliath was defeated.

People around us—friends, family, co-workers, those in authority, church brothers and sisters—will often try to tell us that we need this and that, that we need to do such and such. But when we feel in our hearts that something in that disagrees with what we know from God, we must look beyond the obvious to see the plan of the enemy trying to unfold.

People mean well when they share their opinions. They believe they are guiding us with sound wisdom. But who is the only one that will be held responsible for our actions and obedience? Yes, it comes down to just we ourselves.

David had to take that which Saul said he needed and put it back down on the ground, and leave it behind. People will pressure us into looking the part, being the part, and acting the part they think is right for us. The truth is that part actually has no part in us.

Saul was trying to make David look like something that he was not—a typical soldier. God had a different plan. God will always get the glory when we step our ego out of the picture. It is truly the foolish things of God that will confound the wise every time.

As we look at these truths right now, the Holy Spirit is confirming this word in many lives. Don't ignore Him just now; don't compromise in this moment of revelation. God has a distinctive plan for each of our lives. Right now is a perfect time for each of us to yield to what He is saying within our hearts at this time. Trying to be what other people want is the worst kind of individual misery.

The Relief Valve

Today we face so many pressures that try to force us to fit in with the world around us. We're challenged to look a certain way, act a certain way, talk and be a certain way. We have all this pressure pushing against us on every side every day.

Add to that our dealing with our own personal issues daily, how are we ever able to live a life free from pressure? We are already past the point of exhaustion trying to keep up with crazy work schedules and domestic situations. Pile on some financial issues like bills, house payments or rent, car payments, taxes, bill collectors, groceries…it's a wonder we haven't faded away along the wayside long before now!

With all this pressure coming at us all the time from so many different directions, we have to ask, *where's the relief valve?* Well, there does happen to be one! A relief valve is used to control or limit the pressure in a system or vessel which can build up for a process upset, instrument or equipment failure, or fire. The relief valve is designed or set to open at a predetermined pressure level to protect vessels and other equipment from being subjected to pressures that exceed their design limits. When that set pressure level is exceeded, the relief valve becomes the "path of least resistance" as the valve is forced open and a portion of the fluid is diverted through the auxiliary route.

How many times have we heard someone say, *I'm to the boiling point*? What does that mean? Simply, get as far away as possible from that person! Why? They are getting ready to explode due to the "steam" pressure of their situation building up within them. I believe a person who experiences this level of upset constantly is on the verge of "equipment failure" and a total shutdown. Mental institutions, hospitals, and nursing homes are filled with people who have suffered the consequences of not having a proper relief valve in their lives.

They are getting ready to explode due to the "steam" pressure of their situation building up within them.

Within ourselves, a relief valve must be installed. It doesn't occur automatically. Once it is installed, it cannot be removed. The choice of installation is ours. Proverbs 18:14 speaks to this issue: *The spirit of a man will sustain his infirmity; but a wounded spirit who can bear?* We work out physically to improve our cardiovascular system, to build muscle, to become fit, and to compete. There are many reasons we do this. But if we are not careful, we will fail to exercise our spirit in the same way.

When we deal with emotional, spiritual, and physical issues it doesn't matter how far we can run or how much we can lift. It doesn't matter how good we look in the mirror. That which we are dealing with cannot be combated with that which is carnal. It has to be battled in the spirit. We spend so much time building up our physical bodies, but we neglect to build up the most influential aspect of who we are—our spirits.

It is interesting to take a moment to think about the last time we had to deal with a problem that came with much pressure. When that problem presented itself in our lives, did we flex our physical muscles at it? Did we put on our running shoes and deal with it in the physical realm? No! It's impossible. When has flexing muscles over an empty checkbook ever raised the balance even a penny?

This is why, when trying times arise, it is vital to our survival to have a relief valve in place. One way to do this is to exercise our spirits. There is great value in comparing how much time and effort we spend in the world doing something versus how much time we commit to doing what God wants us to do. Very often, for most of us, the former far exceeds the latter.

What results from this sad imbalance appears in our lives in painful and hurtful ways. We choose to spend so much of our time over in the world where all that pressure comes from and so little of our time with Him

Who can help relieve that pressure. This is insanity! If we are constantly wasting time doing things that are not improving our quality of life, where is the wisdom? Where is the peace?

I heard a pastor say, "If you are too busy to do the things of God, then you are wasting your time." In Ephesians we find a commandment that is still important and worthy of our obedience today:

> [15]See then that ye walk circumspectly, not as fools, but as wise,
> [16]Redeeming the time, because the days are evil.
> [17]Whereforebe ye not unwise, but understanding what the will of the Lord *is*. Ephesians 5:15-17

We are to redeem the time, but what does that really mean? It means *to free from what distresses or harms: to change for the better.* That means making choices that will install a relief valve from the pressurized situations that come to us in life. So many times when we make a change in our circumstances for the better, we also feel a surge in the strength of our spirits. Hmm. Maybe what the Bible says to do is actually true! It is so wise for us to hearken unto the commandments of the Lord. The sad truth is, however, there are so many among us who insist on doing the exact opposite, then wonder why life isn't working out in abundance as God promised.

> [28]Come unto me, all *ye* that labour and are heavy laden, and I will give you rest.
> [29]Take my yoke upon you, and learn of me; for I am meek and lowly in heart: and ye shall find rest unto your souls.
> [30]For my yoke *is* easy, and my burden is light.
> Matthew 11:28-30

Why do we not then do that? Do we find ourselves in a more self-righteous state when we don't? Are we responsible for the calamities facing us, and therefore, it is up to us to carry the load? Paul already told us in Ephesians to walk circumspectly (thinking carefully about possible risks before doing or saying something), and not as fools.

The question always remains for us to answer: *When do we want it to end?* It is solely up to us to obey. God is not going to force Himself on us in any way. He can't force us to do anything we don't want to do. He has already done everything possible to be our relief valve. But if we don't want Him installed in our lives, then we cannot blame Him for our own "equipment failures."

It should be quite obvious, but ask yourself this question: *Who is stronger, the Holy Spirit or me?* In light of this we must be honest and ask,

- How much time do I spend getting filled with the Holy Spirit?
- How much time do I get into the Word of God so it can get into me?
- How much do I esteem others better than myself?
- Are my words and thoughts positive or negative?
- What is the altitude of my attitude?

We don't ask that of ourselves nearly enough. For so many of us, the reply comes down to simply, *I don't have enough time.*

The answer can be found with a few more questions to ask ourselves and answer honestly.

- How much time did I spend watching TV and movies this week?
- How much time did I spend playing golf?
- How much time did I spend fishing?
- How much time did I spend shopping?
- How much time did I spend on my computer? my phone? my tablet?

The truthful answers to these questions will always be nothing more than mere excuses we hide behind. They are completely without merit or validity.

Anything and everything that compromises your focus on what God has told you to do, you must destroy. The Lord had given me a revelation concerning just this:

> The time is short. Judgment is come and we will stand before the Son of Man and we will give account to the Lamb and there will be no one with excuse before the Great I Am.

~~~~~

[1]Brethren, if a man be overtaken in a fault, ye which are spiritual, restore such an one in the spirit of meekness; considering thyself, lest thou also be tempted.
[2]Bear ye one another's burdens, and so fulfill the law of Christ. Galatians 6:1-2

We must be willing to step out of our comfort zone to help somebody else and restore those who have been overtaken in a fault. That's another good question to ask ourselves—when was the last time we did that? Doing so will strengthen our spirits. When that other person experiences victory, we experience victory as well.

The amount of time we spend in God's word and being a doer of His word will reflect directly onto how much pressure is relieved from our lives. It is a big deception from the enemy that so many of us today try to find some other way of being and doing than God's way. How can we possibly know more than our God? We have become so foolish in doing things our own way and missing out on the joy of walking in obedience to Him!

Living a Godly life is a vital part to this process of keeping the relief valve in place and working properly. When we fail to do so we see clearly how ineffective a weak spirit can be. Just like Proverbs tells us, a wounded spirit is not able to bear or deal with the things that harm us emotionally, mentally, physically, or spiritually. When our spirit is weak our whole being is weak. And in those times the enemy loves to come against us because it is so much easier for him to set up a stronghold in our lives.

That is why a continual fellowship with the Holy Spirit is so extremely necessary to our being victorious in this world. We cannot afford to be distracted from drawing ourselves away unto our Heavenly Father. We must lay aside all the distractions to embrace Him Who loves to pour out His many wonderful blessings upon His people!

We have only to just come to Him. The invitation is open to one and all. None is exempted. The banqueting table is prepared for us along with His banner of love over us. So the ultimate question remains: will we choose to accept His invitation or simply deny the possibility of any hope of salvation from our tribulation?

Please pray this with me:

> Heavenly Father, I thank You that You have never left me nor have You abandoned me emotionally. In You alone are my strength, my love, my joy, and my peace. I thank You that it is You that makes wars to cease. Even though it may seem I am in a helpless place right now, I know that You still possess it altogether. I thank You for perfecting that which concerns me. Though I walk through the midst of trouble, persecution, darkness, and pressure You are the One Who revives me by Your great grace.

> I ask that you would give glory to Yourself as You have already provided deliverance in my situation. I do not look unto man, but I lift up my eyes unto the hills from where my help comes for I know that my help comes from You, Lord. Thank You for coming quickly to my rescue and for manifesting Your power to me so that I will walk in Your Word in absolute victory.

> According to Your Own Word, Lord, I cast all of my cares, including burdens and pressures, upon you. (Tell every one of them to the Lord and refuse to pick them up again.) In exchange I joyfully take upon me Your yoke and burden for they are truly easy and light.

> I thank You, Holy Spirit, for being my Comforter by manifesting the fruit of the Spirit abundantly within my mind, soul, spirit, and body. I thank You, Jesus, that I have found grace in Your sight. Thank You for Your strength and victory in the middle of this fight.

> In Jesus' Mighty Name, I praise You! And I thank You! Amen.

About the Author

Rusty Moore was born in Kirksville, Missouri, in 1975 and was raised on a farm most of his life after the family moved to the Trenton, Missouri area. But following the family's farming tradition was not meant to be. In the summer of 1995 at the age of nineteen, Rusty dedicated his life to Jesus, and he will tell you, "My life has never been the same since!"

Two years later he followed the leading of the Lord and moved from northern Missouri southward to Branson, Missouri. It was during his time in the Branson area that the realization became clear—God was preparing him for His ministry.

In the third grade Rusty was introduced to drumming and took lessons for a short time. Though his interest in playing drums continued, the funds to continue the lessons did not. It never occurred to him that God would take those few drum lessons and use him in His church. But God being God, in 2005, He opened a door of opportunity for Rusty to use his passion for the drums to play for Him in churches and conferences in the Branson area.

Shortly after this drumming began, another opportunity arose for him to speak at a local church. That was where the door swung wide open to God's true purpose in his life—preaching the gospel of Jesus. He became the youth pastor of a local church in Branson, also preaching on occasion in the absence of the pastors.

The revelations and the anointing that the Lord has placed within Rusty grew as he prepared messages. Soon he realized the Lord was calling on him to begin writing and sharing with others the good news of His good things.

Rusty is the father of two beautiful children, daughter Jaden and son Evan. Shortly after his birth, Evan was diagnosed with autism. For Rusty, the pressures of dealing with internal family struggles strengthened his faith in God and in the purpose that God had chosen for him.

In 2015 he watched his father pass away from cancer. Again, the pressures that came after that loss only testified more strongly to the purpose of God's revelation in his life. In the overwhelming evidence of today's pressure and stress that exists within the modern day family threatening to tear it apart, Rusty's God-inspired revelation of *fighting for the family* propels him to strengthen not only the church, but also the family home.

Rusty is following the leading of the Lord and fulfilling the call of God on his life. He continues to write the revelations of the Lord as He gives them, and is available to minister when called upon.

Contact Information

If you would like to contact Rusty for further information or to discuss the possibility of him coming to speak and minister at your church or group, you may reach him using the information below.

Email: ChristianTaskForce@gmail.com
Website: www. rustydmoore.com
Facebook: www.facebook.com/christiantaskforceunit/